Career Development Theories in Practice

Julia Yates

trotman | t

Career Development Theories in Practice

This first edition published in 2024 by Trotman, an imprint of Trotman Indigo Publishing Ltd, 18e Charles Street, Bath, BA1 1HX

© Trotman Indigo Publishing Ltd 2024

Author: Julia Yates

British Library Cataloguing in Publication Data
A catalogue record for this book is available from the British Library.

Paperback ISBN 978 1 911724 30 8
Hardback ISBN 978 1 911724 32 2

Printed and bound in the UK by Ashford Colour Press, Gosport, PO13 0FW

All details in this book were correct at the time of going to press. To keep up-to-date with all the latest news and updates and to access the online resources that accompany this book, use the QR code or visit **trotman. co.uk/pages/career-development-theories-in-practice-resources**

Contents

Figures

About the author

Dr Julia Yates is Associate Professor and Deputy Head of Psychology at City, University of London, where she teaches the award-winning MSc in Organisational Psychology.

Julia specialises in the development of individuals within their careers and teaches career development, coaching psychology and learning and training. Her research interests are in career decision-making and the career paths of those facing particular barriers. Julia is passionate about the links between academia and practice, and speaks and writes widely on the practical applications of career development theories and research.

Julia is a Chartered Psychologist of the British Psychological Society (BPS) and a full member of its Division of Occupational Psychology. She is also a Senior Fellow of Advance HE and a Fellow of the National Institute of Career Education and Counselling (NICEC)

Julia has written widely on careers, including the much respected *The Career Coaching Handbook*, published by Routledge in 2022.

Acknowledgements

First, I would like to thank the marvellous career professionals who agreed to let me interview them for my study on career theories. That's where it started, and your stories and examples of using theories in your practice restored my slightly wavering devotion to career theories and filled me with admiration, so thank you for so generously giving me your time and for being such inspirational figures. The CDI was obviously pivotal in making this happen, so thanks to the whole team, but particularly Claire Johnson. Claire, you did a very good job of making me put my money where my mouth is, encouraging me to stop talking and start writing. Thank you for that. I was very pleased to be able to include such a good range of practical case studies in the book, and my thanks go to each of the contributors for sharing your expertise with the profession. My colleagues at NICEC and at City always push me onwards and upwards and somehow make me feel able to do things, and my students, every single year, make my work meaningful and motivate me to strive to be a better version of myself. So I thank every one of you from across the years. Finally of course, my wonderful family: Jack, Ted and Hugh, you make it all make sense.

To my mother

Foreword

Julia Yates writes with such passion and enthusiasm about career development theories that readers of this book will have 'light bulb moments' when understanding the different career development theories and how using relevant ones in practice leads to deeper understanding, greater confidence and more effective practice with clients.

If you are studying to become a career development professional, this book is essential reading as it introduces what career development theories are, categorises a range of the most useful theories into different themes, explains them clearly and then shows how to use them in practice.

For experienced career development professionals, the book will act as both a refresher and an introduction to theories that have been developed since you qualified. Its accessible format means that it is an excellent source of continuous professional development as it encourages you to reflect on your own practice through the lens of career development theories. It is also a very useful source of information when advocating for the value of career development work and explaining its theoretical foundations.

If, like me, you have been fortunate and have attended one of Julia's sessions on career development theories in practice, you are likely to have been sad when it finished and could happily have listened to Julia for much longer. This book is the answer to your wishes, as Julia's engaging style can be heard throughout.

For the last 30 years of my 40-year career in the sector I have been involved in designing, delivering and developing many of the initial qualifications and supporting the continuous professional development needs of the sector. I have no hesitation in recommending this book as essential reading for all career development professionals, anyone interested in joining the sector or if you want to know more about career development theories and the impact that their effective use can have.

Claire Johnson, RCDP and CDI, ICCI and NICEC Fellow
CDI Head of Professional Development and Standards
October 2024

Part One

Introduction

Overview

In this section, I want to introduce the book, explain why I decided to put it together and highlight what you will gain from it. I will then give an overview of the content, outlining what the different chapters will cover, and give some suggestions on how you might want to use it.

Introduction

I spend a lot of my life immersed in career development theories. I find them interesting. I enjoy finding out how different people understand the whole idea of a career, and I like thinking about my own career development through the lens of the different theories. I often use theories within my own career conversations and find that they enhance my practice and boost my confidence. But learning about career theories and working out how to apply them in practice takes time. I am not a full-time career professional – I have the luxury of having a university job alongside my career coaching practice, which allows me to spend time reading and learning about different approaches. I certainly didn't have the time to do this when I was a full-time careers adviser, and my guess is that many of you are in a similar position. In this book, I want to try and share what I've learnt with you in a digestible, practitioner-oriented way. I hope that you will find it an accessible way to learn about the theories and how you can use them in your practice.

Learning outcomes

There are five learning outcomes for the book.

By the end of the book, you will:

- understand what a theory is and what career development theories are;
- be aware of different categories of career development theories;

- appreciate how career development theories can add value to your practice;
- be familiar with 25 different career theories and how to use them in practice;
- have reflected on your own practice through the lens of career development theories.

Content

The book is divided into two parts. Part One offers some general information to make sure we all share a common understanding of what career theories are, the value they can add and ways that they can be incorporated into career practice.

In Chapter 1, I will try to define *what a theory is*. In Chapter 2, we look at *career development theories* and the different ways people categorise them. In Chapter 3, we focus on the research that shows *what value can career development theories add?* In Chapter 4, I give some general suggestions on *how to use theories in one-to-one practice career conversations*. And in Chapter 5, we focus on *how to use theories in career education programmes*.

In Part Two, we turn to some specific theories. The theories are grouped around some typical issues that our clients bring to us, and I hope this will show where and when you can use the different theories in your work. Within each chapter, I will introduce three or four theories, explain them and give some specific suggestions about using them in practice.

In Chapter 6, we focus on three *theories to explain career influences*. We start with Bill Law's theory of *Community Interaction*, which looks specifically at the people who shape our career thinking. We move on to Patton and McMahon's *Systems Theory Framework of Career Development*, which offers a comprehensive analysis of all the different factors and features that influence our career plans, and then we look at Gottfredson's theory of *Circumscription and Compromise*, which highlights the way the world around young children influences their ideas of the kinds of jobs that will be suitable for them.

In Chapter 7, we highlight three *theories to help clients with their emotions*. We start with Bandura's *Self-efficacy Theory*, which explains how we can help clients boost their self-confidence. Then, we move to *Acceptance and Commitment Therapy*, which offers techniques to help people to change the impact that their negative thoughts and feelings have on their behaviour. Finally, we look at Seligman's *PERMA Model*, which describes five pillars of wellbeing.

In Chapter 8, the focus turns to *theories to help clients to take ownership of their own career planning*. The first theory is Mitchell et al.'s much-beloved descriptive theory of *Planned Happenstance*, which highlights the role of chance in career paths and offers us advice on how to improve our chances of identifying and capitalising on chance events. We then move to two theories by Mark Savickas. We start with his *Career Construction Theory* that aims to combine some of the most useful aspects of well-established approaches to career development and helps people to navigate contemporary careers. We then look at *Career AdaptAbilities*, which focuses on one concept from Career Construction Theory and helps people to build the competencies needed to negotiate their way through the complexities of modern work.

In Chapter 9, we will look at four *theories to explain the process of career decision-making*. First, I describe Lent, Brown and Hackett's *Social Cognitive Career Theory*, which gives an overview of how career decisions are made, focusing on the pivotal role of confidence and combining personal and environmental factors. Then, we turn to Kahneman's *System 1 and System 2 Decision-Making*, which is a psychological analysis of the cognitive processes of decision-making. We then look at Verbruggen and De Vos' *Career Inaction Theory*, which highlights where people often get stuck in their career planning. Finally, there is my own *Real-World Model of Graduate Career Decision Making*, which describes how young people choose their first job when they finish education.

Chapter 10 puts the spotlight on three *theories that can help to enhance self-awareness*. First, we focus on the idea of *career success* and show how the differences between objective and subjective career success can reveal our values. We then look at Holland's *RIASEC hexagon*, which helps people to identify their career interests. Finally, we focus on Chen's theory of *career self-determination*, which describes key aspects of career motivation.

In Chapter 11, we examine three theories that can help to explain *the career paths of people who are marginalised* or who face particular barriers or discrimination in the workplace. First, we look at Blustein's *Psychology of Working Theory*, which shows how marginalisation and limited economic resources make people less likely to end up in 'decent work'. We then look at Mainiero and Sullivan's *Kaleidoscope Career Model*, which explores different career motivations of men and women at different times in their careers. Finally, we will cover Arulmani's *Cultural Preparedness Process Model*, which analyses the way our culture informs our understanding of work and career.

In Chapter 12, we look at *theories that can be used to enhance employability skills*. We cover Arthur and Fillippi's *Intelligent Career Framework*, which identifies three personal resources that can help people to navigate their careers. Then we move on to Luthans' idea of *Psychological Capital*, which focuses on four psychological resources that have been shown to combine together to enhance workplace performance. And finally, we explore the three intertwined constructs within Fugate, Ashforth and Kinicki's *Psycho-Social Framework of Employability*.

In the last chapter, we focus on *theories that can help us to understand career transitions*. We look first at Schlossberg's *Transition Theory*, which aims to explain how people adapt to transitions. We then turn to Akkerman's idea of *Career Shocks* and show the impact that events, positive and negative, can have on people's career thinking and action. Finally, we end on a positive note, exploring Waters and Strauss' idea of *Post-Job-loss Career Growth*.

The chapters in Part One are designed to be covered in order, but in Part Two you might want to pick and choose where you start and what you cover. I want the book to be useful, and it makes sense to focus on the aspects that seem most readily applicable in your work.

The terminology used to describe our profession has been the subject of some debate over the years. In this book, I tend to use the phrase 'career professional' and talk about 'career practice', but I am writing to all of you – whether you call yourself a careers adviser, career coach, career counsellor, career consultant or anything else. The theories aim to help anyone who is making a career decision or, actually, anyone who has a career, so if you are working with clients and supporting them with their career development, then the theories could be useful, whatever you call yourself and whatever client group you work with.

I have mentioned already that I want the book to be accessible. I want you to be able to just read through it and understand the key points and the value that each theory can add without too much effort or the need to have a dictionary by your side, so I have tried hard to make it readable. The content of the book is rigorously academic – every topic is well researched, grounded in empirical research and based on peer-reviewed publications. But to make it more digestible, it's light on references. I have glossed over some of the criticisms and nuances of the theories and sometimes changed the language and simplified the ideas a bit. I make no apologies for this – there are plenty of more detailed texts that you can go to if you want to delve deep. I do offer suggestions for further reading at the end of the book if one of the theories catches your eye and you would like to know more. But this book is not aimed at academics. It's aimed at practitioners, and it's all about making the theories straightforward to understand and easy to apply. The book is designed to be useful to you wherever you are in your own career journey. If you are just starting out as a career professional and are currently training, the book could be a useful introduction to the practical applications of a range of theories. If you have recently qualified, it might give you some new practical ideas for applying the theories that you have learnt. If you are a more experienced career professional, it could be a useful refresher and might include some more recent theories that perhaps you didn't come across in your initial training. I very much hope that you can find some ideas that resonate with you and some practical suggestions that you can use to add value to your clients.

Key takeaways

The book offers an easily digestible, practically oriented overview of a range of career theories.

Part One covers theories and their use in practice in general terms.

Part Two focuses on a range of specific theories.

Chapter 1
What is a theory?

Overview

In this chapter, I want to start with some definitions. I will try to unpick what a theory is and how it differs from a model or framework. I will then explain what I mean by career development theories.

Defining a theory turns out to be not as straightforward as you might imagine. In ordinary conversation, the idea of a theory is a sort of working hypothesis. I have a theory about why my children won't tidy their bedrooms; I have a theory about why reality television is so popular. I also have lots of theories about work. I have a theory about why so many people are drawn to careers in law and a theory about why girls generally don't study engineering. These aren't theories in any formal or academic sense, but they are my own attempts to make sense of something I can't immediately understand. And it is this that is at the heart of a theory. A theory answers a question 'why' — it offers an explanation of something that, on the surface, seems odd or contradictory or is unexplained. A theory that explains 'why' will also, usually, have some predictive power: if it explains why something has happened in the past, it can probably also offer some predictions for why something might happen in the future. So a theory explains and predicts.

Academic theories are broadly the same, but they are defined a bit more tightly; although even here, the academic community hasn't quite yet agreed on a definition. Some academics talk about theories having to be either falsifiable or generalisable, but others disagree, arguing that being able to disprove a theory is only relevant to a research context, and that theories can be quite context-specific.

Confusing us yet further, some academics argue that rather than being a binary construct (i.e. something either is a theory or is not), it is more of a continuum. This highlights that there is a process of theory building that starts with some ideas and gradually evolves into a theory, so you can then identify emergent theories, weak theories and strong theories. A strong theory isn't necessarily a good one. A strong theory is one that clearly meets the criteria for being a theory – so it explains and predicts; this is about definitions. A good theory is simple, general, testable and accurate; this is about quality. Let us delve a little deeper and think about what we mean by a good theory.

Compelling theories are, at heart, compelling stories. They start, as all good stories do, with a conflict or a problem: how do people make good career choices? Why are some people's career ideas narrow? Why is it that some people don't feel confident about their skills? A theory then identifies its main characters – or main constructs: parental influence, gender, values, self-efficacy and such like. It defines a setting for the story – defining the perspective of the theory – whether that is a psychological perspective, a sociological one, a focus on career learning or on cognitive processes. Finally, the story (or theory) needs to offer an event sequence – how the different elements or constructs fit together: how growing up as a girl determines the kinds of options you feel are suitable and how that then influences your career choices; how feedback has an impact on your confidence which determines how you perform in job interviews.

So a theory explains and predicts, and shows how different relevant constructs fit together. What about a model? Models and theories both try to offer a simplified, small-scale representation of something. But where a model can simply describe what is going on, a theory has the added requirement to explain and predict. Finally, then, what about a framework? The terms 'framework' and 'model' are often used interchangeably, but they are technically distinct. A framework is more practical than a model – a model represents the key components, but a framework offers a structure for actually putting something into practice.

In this book, I have deliberately chosen to be a bit relaxed about my definition of a theory. I am less concerned by technical definitions and more concerned about offering you something that you are going to find useful. In Part Two of the book I will be introducing a number of models and frameworks alongside some more traditionally defined theories. The models that I have chosen do usually link closely with formal theories, offering a practical approach for using the theories in practice. The Career AdaptAbilities model, for example, is very closely linked with Savickas' theory of Career Construction. But my aim is to offer a book that is useful, and sometimes a model or framework might be just what you need.

One final definition I want to leave you with comes from an organisational scholar called Weick, who says that a good theory *explains, predicts and delights*. That feels like quite an ambitious goal for a book on career theories, and I'm not sure that I can promise that you will all get quite such pleasure out of a theory! But even if I can't guarantee delight, I am going to try to show how theories can help you to understand your clients' situations more quickly and more deeply, and make your career conversations more effective.

Key takeaways

Theories aim to explain and predict things.

A model is a simplified representation of the key components of a phenomenon.

A framework offers a structure for putting an idea or theory into practice.

Chapter 2
What kinds of career development theories are there?

Overview

In this chapter, I examine some of the types of theories that we can use in career practice. I offer a number of different ways to categorise career development theories, including the traditional chronological approach, metaphors and the practical categorisation that is used to structure this book.

Career professionals can make good use of a range of different types of theory. One group of theories are those that help us to structure or conduct our career conversations. These might include things like Egan's three-stage Skilled Helper model, the GROW framework or Ali and Graham's four-stage career counselling model. They could also include broader approaches such as humanism, solution-focused approaches or cognitive behavioural approaches. These might be described as *models of guidance*, or practitioner or coaching approaches. These approaches are covered extensively elsewhere, and actually, the evidence suggests that they are generally very well used in career practice, so we won't be looking at them in this book.

The group of theories that we will be exploring here are career development theories. These theories focus on the *process of career development*: what our clients are going through, rather than what we as practitioners are doing. The boundaries between groups of theories are a little muddy. Many of the career development theories come with their own models for practice, and it's also fair to say that some of the most useful ones I will cover in this book aren't even career-specific – many were originally developed in other fields and adapted to a career context later on. But broadly speaking, the focus of this book is on career development theories and how to use them in practice.

There are dozens of career development theories, and dozens (maybe hundreds) of other theories which help to explain different aspects of career development. The earliest career theory commonly cited is Parsons' famous conceptualisation of career planning, published back in 1909 (1: learn about yourself, 2: research occupations, 3: apply 'true reasoning' and voila, your perfect career) and new theories have been published every decade since.

An argument is sometimes made that we now have enough career theories. What is needed now is more of a consolidation – a focus on bringing the theories together, refining them or providing more empirical evidence to back them up, and more techniques for using them in practice. This does seem to make a lot of sense, particularly perhaps to practitioners who are already awash with things to read; yet the theories do seem to keep coming.

One of the reasons for the proliferation of theories is that career development is so complex and so broad. Some theories aim to offer an explanation of the whole process of career development, but most theoreticians pick one aspect to look at. They might focus on what influences career choices, or the cognitive processes involved. They might look at different demographic groups, career trajectories or different life stages. More theories then emerge because of the different philosophical positions that the authors hold, and some academics end up developing theories that are just very subtly different from others because they are so immersed in the detail that they end up quite convinced that their approach is meaningfully distinct and significantly better. One other complication is that the world keeps on changing. We are now considering post-Covid careers, hybrid working, green jobs and trans issues at work – none of which would have been in Parsons' mind back in 1909.

Between them, the theories probably offer a pretty comprehensive account of the process of career development. But while this is helpful to some degree, in that each aspect gets a thorough treatment, it does leave us with the challenge of integrating the theories – putting them back together. Our clients are complex people whose many facets are inextricably fused together to make a single unique whole person; understanding a client piece by piece doesn't always help us to build up the whole picture.

The landscape of career theories is vast and complex, but each theory has something to add. Finding a useful way to categorise the theories is therefore important. If we can find a useful way to divide the whole landscape of theories into a small number of groups, this will help us to make sense of them, remember them and work out how they fit together. Different writers have divided the theories up in different ways. The most common way is to describe them chronologically.

A chronological account of career theories might go something like this:

> The earliest theories were developed in the 1950s by the differentialist psychologists such as Holland, and Dawis and Loftquist. These approaches assumed that the best way to make a career choice was to match particular individual characteristics with particular job characteristics. Next came the developmentalists (e.g. Super) from the 1960s who considered the idea that people changed and developed throughout their lives and therefore had different career needs and requirements as they got older. The sociologists (e.g. Roberts, and Hodgkinson and Sparkes) in the 1970s and 80s acknowledged the important role that context had in career development. In the 1990s the focus shifted towards career learning and scholars such as Krumboltz and Law identified the processes through which people learned about careers. More recently, in the 21st century, the most popular approach has been a constructivist one, which assumes that individuals develop their own individual understanding of career development through their interaction with the world – Savickas is a pioneer in this tradition.

The chronological approach offers an interesting historical context but seems to imply that there is some sense of progress where older, less useful theories have been superseded by better, more recent theories. In truth, some of the older theories are still extremely relevant, and a comprehensive understanding of career development really requires the old as well as the new. Another problem with this chronological model is that its fairly rigid categorisation of dates and approaches can make it hard to find a home for some theories which have been developed more recently and for those which seem to straddle two groups.

Another useful categorisation comes from Patton and McMahon, who divide theories into those about content (the things that influence career choices), those about process (how career choice happens) and those that cover both content and process. Theories that focus on content include those that focus on matching – such as Holland's theory of career interests and theories that look at individual characteristics such as values or personality. Theories about process might include Gottfredson's theory of circumscription and compromise and Super's work on life stages. Examples of theories that cover both include Lent and colleagues' Social Cognitive Career Theory and Savickas' Career Construction Theory.

Inkson's categorisation of career theories focuses on the metaphors that are used in career theories. He developed a taxonomy of career theories using nine different metaphors that are often used in the career development literature. These include career as the product of inheritance (e.g. Gottfredson's circumscription and compromise), career as a series of roles (Super's life career rainbow), career as a journey (Arthur's boundaryless career) and career as fit (Schein's career anchors).

These different categorisations all make sense and all have their place. But in this book, I am taking yet another approach. The purpose of this book is to show how the theories can be used in practice, so I thought it made sense to group the theories based on the career-related challenges they address – that way you can relate the theories directly to the client context.

Clients bring different kinds of career issues and dilemmas to us: emotional, cognitive and behavioural. We might, for example, work with clients to help them with their confidence or levels of anxiety, to develop their self-awareness or understanding about how to make a career choice or perhaps we might help them to take more ownership or develop the skills needed to secure the job they want.

Each chapter in this book focuses on a particular type of challenge that our clients bring to us and offers a few theories that might be particularly relevant to each type of challenge. I am hoping that this particular categorisation will make it easier to work out when you might want to use each particular theory in your practice.

Key takeaways

There are many career development theories, which focus on different aspects of the career development process or might be underpinned by different philosophical assumptions.

New theories keep coming as the world changes and as we learn more about it.

Theories have been categorised in different ways, including chronologically and themed on the basis of metaphors.

In this book, I have categorised them on the basis of client challenges.

Chapter 3
What value can career development theories add?

Overview

In this section, I offer an overview of some of the key benefits that career development theory can bring to career practice, looking specifically at the contribution that they can make to practitioners, practice and clients.

Introduction

The goal of this entire book is to try to help career development professionals to use career theories within their practice and in this chapter I want to give an overview of the value that they can add. No doubt you have decided to read this book because you are already at least somewhat convinced that theories can add value, so I know I am preaching to the converted here. But I do think it's worth unpicking the range of contributions that theories can make, not just to reassure you that you are not wasting your time, but also to encourage you to think about theories broadly, and to look out for opportunities to use them in different ways at different times.

The details in this chapter have come from a few different sources. Some are from my own practice. I have been a career professional for 25 years and have worked with all sorts of clients. I draw on theories in various different ways in my career coaching conversations, and have included here some of the ways in which I see them add value. Most of the ideas, however, are from other people. A few years ago I conducted a piece of research with careers advisers in the UK. I spoke to 30 self-confessed theory-geeks about how they used theories in their practice and the value that they felt the theories added to their work. I found their stories inspirational and the ideas in this chapter are mostly drawn from our discussions.

The benefits of theory-informed practice

The benefits of theory-informed practice can broadly be grouped into three: deeper understanding, greater confidence and more effective practice.

Benefit one: Deeper understanding

- *Insights for practitioners*

First and foremost, theories can help us to understand our clients and their stories more quickly and at a deeper level. As your client starts to tell their story, bells start ringing in your head. You link different aspects of their story to different theories you know about, and you can start to build up an understanding of where they might be coming from and what they might have experienced. This leads to greater empathy as you begin to see their story from more angles and get a more in-depth understanding of their experiences. Theories can also help you to know which questions to ask. Asking the right questions can help you to build your relationship with your clients, as you show that you understand their situation, they can lead to more efficient and effective conversations, and they can help to move the conversation in the most useful direction.

- *Insights for our clients*

It is sometimes really valuable to share the theories explicitly with clients as this can lead directly to insights for them. Some theories might be a bit complicated to describe in a short conversation, but a brief overview or even a quick sketch might be easily incorporated. Theories are there to explain things, and using them to explain your clients' experiences to themselves can be enormously revealing and extremely valuable.

> **Practice tip**
>
> Although theories can very often help you to understand your client better, one thing to guard against is making assumptions. It can be tempting to make a connection between a client's story and a particular theory early on in the conversation, but the risk here is that you assume that you understand their experience and then you stop listening. Theories can help you to relate to your client's story, but it will be a rare occasion when a single theory maps completely onto your client's experience. Remembering that no theory will apply perfectly, and keeping a number of different theories in your mind at once can help with this.

Benefit two: Greater confidence

Theory-informed practice boosts confidence in a number of ways.

- *Confidence in your professional choices*

Knowledge of theories can make practitioners feel more confident that they are doing the right things and going in the right direction. If you are basing your career workshops on a tried and tested theory you can feel confident that you are covering the key topics; if you suggest an exercise to a client that comes from a theoretical approach, you can feel sure that it is a sensible choice.

- *Confidence in your professionalism*

We all develop our own theories about our clients, about careers and about the world of work. Finding a theory that maps onto something that we have already observed can make us feel very positive about our own understanding, and seeing a theory in a client's story can make us feel confident that we really know what we are talking about.

- *Credibility with stakeholders*

It can feel like an uphill struggle to convince some of the people that we work with that we are the highly skilled, well-trained experts that we are. Mentioning that our work is underpinned by a strong theory base clearly demonstrates our professionalism. Referencing theories with clients, teachers, senior leaders and managers can give an immediate boost to our credibility, demonstrating that actually, it's not that easy to be a career professional.

- *Validation for clients*

Clients often come to us with low levels of confidence and high levels of anxiety. It's common to see clients who feel that they have failed or let their families down, or who feel that they are lagging behind their peers. A powerful way to make them feel more positive is to share with them a theory that reflects or explains their situation. This shows them that they are not alone, that their situation is not out of the ordinary and that what they have been going through is 'a thing'. It is amazing what a relief this can be, as the theory normalises their experience and validates their choices.

Benefit three: More effective practice

The two points above – deeper understanding and more confidence – can in themselves lead directly to better practice but in addition, theories can contribute to our professional planning and reflective practice.

- *Planning*

Theories can be used to help us to plan interventions and can help to make sure that the content and approach that we choose is as effective as possible.

- *Reflective practice*

Theories can be a useful lens through which to reflect on your practice. You could consider a client and think about their situation through a number of different theoretical lenses, conceptualising their story through one or two different theories. As well as allowing you to reflect on your clients and your own practice, this approach can encourage you to be a little more self-compassionate: the theories can show how hard the whole process is for your clients, and can remind you that there is a limit on what you should expect yourself to achieve.

THEORIES FOR REFLECTION

David Winter

When you're using theories for reflection, you obviously have to start with getting to grips with the theory itself – working out what the theory says, what the key assumptions are. But one thing I would say is, don't sweat whether you've really understood it properly or not. It's easy to get hung up on whether you accurately understand the details of the theory, but for the purposes of reflection that doesn't necessarily matter. Even if you have technically misunderstood the theory, as long as it's giving you a different perspective on the client or your interaction, it's still useful. If it helps you to become aware of something you weren't aware of at the time, then it's serving its purpose in reflection.

One thing I often do with a theory is to turn it into a set of default questions. I ask myself, what questions would be at the forefront of my mind if I assumed that this theory was true? So, for example, if you believed that Circumscription and Compromise was a complete and accurate description of reality for a client, you would tend to ask yourself about the career options that a client was not even looking at because they had labelled them in their early life as inappropriate for someone of their gender or social background. You'd be looking out for the options they had labelled as desirable but inaccessible to them and trying to identify what those inaccessible options said about the client's ideal career values. If you review your interaction with a client with these issues at the front of your mind, you may notice something that you didn't notice at the time. You may spot instances where you could have pursued an unexplored line of enquiry with the client.

One of the key things about using theories in practice is that even if you don't engage with theories, you have a theory. We are theory-making creatures and part of what we're trying to do in life is to make sense of our world and create meaning. We do this through coming up with our own theories about what is going on. So with every experience you have with a client, you'll be building up your own implicit theory about how things work and what's important. And, unless you kind of have something to compare that implicit theory with, it will influence your actions without you knowing it. And so that's a key value that theoretical reflection can bring, to give you that external perspective.

Key takeaways

Career development theories can be useful for practitioners, for clients and for practice.

They can deepen our understanding of our clients, leading to more empathy and sharper questions, and can lead to insights for clients themselves.

They can boost our confidence in our own practice and our professional credibility in others' eyes.

They can normalise and validate clients' own choices or experiences.

They can be used to guide practice, suggesting a direction for the conversation, an exercise to try or a framework for career education.

They can be used as a lens for reflective practice, allowing us to think more deeply about our clients and our choices.

Chapter 4
Career theories in one-to-one career conversations

Overview

In this section, we will focus on using career development theories in one-to-one work. We will look at the different ways they can be used and I'll give some specific examples which I hope you will be able to apply in your own practice.

Introduction

We saw in the previous chapter that understanding and using career development theories in practice can lead to a number of benefits to us professionally and to our clients. In this chapter we're going to delve a bit deeper to think about how they can be particularly used in one-to-one work. In Part Two of the book I'll be offering some theory-specific ideas for use in practice, but here I want to give some broader tips that could help you to use any theory in your one-to-one conversations.

I'm going to show how to use theories in five different ways:

- To help you understand and empathise with your clients.
- To give a language to help you both to articulate thoughts and feelings.
- To normalise and validate clients' thoughts, feelings and behaviours.
- To guide the conversation – informing your questions and suggesting specific tools.
- As a tool for reflection.

I'm also going to talk about how, when and whether to share details of the theory explicitly with clients and how to choose which theory to use, and I'll end with a couple of warnings – traps that I've fallen into in my own practice, that you might want to guard against.

Theories in one-to-one practice

1. *To help you to understand and empathise with your clients.*

We know that career planning is difficult and in general most of us are pretty empathic with the challenges our clients are facing. But knowledge of theories can help us to be even more understanding of our clients because it can help us to see where they have come from. One example is Career Inaction Theory, which I talk more about in Chapter 9. In my practice I have found myself getting a bit frustrated on occasions with clients who just aren't moving forwards. A knowledge of Career Inaction Theory has helped me to be a bit more patient as it reminds me that actually, moving forwards can be really scary, overwhelming and difficult. I might share the theory explicitly with the client – if they are feeling impatient or frustrated with themselves over their own lack of progress, it can help them to be a little more self-compassionate. Or I might just keep it in my own head – a useful reminder to me to be a bit more understanding.

2. *Using tools to give a language to help you both to articulate thoughts and feelings.*

One of the most valuable things about any kind of counselling intervention is that it offers clients an opportunity to voice their thoughts and feelings. This process of putting words to whatever is going round in their heads allows them to make their abstract ideas concrete and refine their thinking. Thoughts can be a bit floaty and ephemeral – a general sense of something, rather than a clear, specific idea. Often, particularly when the thoughts are complex or novel, it is only through articulating them, that they become real and meaningful. The very process of putting a word to something helps you to understand what you yourself actually mean.

The words used in theories have generally been very thoughtfully considered – carefully selected because they mean precisely what the author wanted them to mean, and as a result, they often include exactly the right word. If you can offer your client the words from a theory (e.g. – *'it sounds like you weren't given any autonomy'* or *'I can see that your community has really influenced you'*) it can sometimes help your client to understand what they themselves mean.

The concepts that are covered by theories can be similarly spot-on and sometimes theories can offer a really helpful framework to help clients to understand themselves. One that often helps people to understand their dissatisfaction with either their current or a previous position, is Self-Determination Theory which identifies three key reasons that explain a lack of motivation (Chapter 10). This is a very wide research theory that has been shown to be consistent in all sorts of different contexts, with all sorts of different kinds of people, and I find that it generally resonates really well with people – offering the right words and concepts to reflect exactly why they felt so unmotivated.

3. *To normalise and validate clients' thoughts, feelings and behaviour.*

Career paths are highly individualised – each of us carves out our own unique path. The whole process of career development can be quite difficult and clients often come to see us when things haven't gone quite the way they had hoped. It's not uncommon for clients to feel that they have been less successful than they had expected in their careers, and to feel that they alone are struggling, or are somehow doing less well, or finding it all more difficult than others. In these circumstances, it can be enormously validating for them to know that there is a theory that covers their situation. The very existence of the theory shows that their experience is widely shared, and far from being something that they alone have felt, their situation is *a thing*. You can often really see a physical relief in clients when you share a theory, as it instantly reduces some of their self-blame or recrimination and boosts their self-esteem.

Planned Happenstance (Chapter 8) is a theory that explains how messy careers are and highlights the influence of luck and chance opportunities. The power of this theory lies in the way that it contradicts society's received wisdom about career planning, which often focuses on the importance of having a career goal and a five-year plan. Clients who don't have a clear goal or a five-year plan can feel inadequate about their lack of direction, but when they hear that Planned Happenstance is a tried and tested theory that reflects how many people actually navigate their careers, this can make them feel really reassured about their own approach.

4. *Theories can be used to help guide the conversations.*

A theory can help you to develop a working hypothesis about what is going on for your client, and you can then test this hypothesis very gently with them. For example, you might be working with a client who is struggling to get a job. Your thoughts might turn to some of the employability frameworks (we cover these in more detail in Chapter 12). Perhaps your client is frustrated because they know that they have exactly the right skills to do the job, but for some reason they just aren't breaking through. You might bring the Intelligent Career Framework to mind and think about the three core elements and the importance of understanding your own motivation, having the right skillset and knowing the right people. You might explain to your client that there is a framework that suggests that all three of these elements are important, and ask them to rate themselves on each. Perhaps they identify that they are indeed strong on the 'knowing how' aspect, but perhaps they are less able to articulate their own motivation, and if so, you can then focus your conversation, productively, on this aspect. Sharing the theory allows them to self-assess – it's your judgement that leads you to pick out a particular theory, but it's your client who confirms whether it resonates. If your hunch is right, then sharing the theory could lead to a useful conversation. If not, that's fine too – you just move onto something else.

5. *Theories can be used to help you reflect on your conversations afterwards.*

Sometimes, career conversations are straightforward. The client comes with a problem, you ask insightful questions, and empathically and skilfully, you get them to identify options and decide on some action points; they leave with a spring in their step, eternally grateful to you for getting them to see things so clearly. Other times things don't work quite so well. These can be the conversations we ruminate on – wondering why we weren't able to get through to a client, or why they seemed to be committed to such an unhelpful course of action, or don't seem to be moving forwards. Theories can be a really useful lens to help us to reflect on the conversations and the clients. You can ask yourself which theories might explain your client's behaviour, or question which assumptions were going on in your own head during the conversation. Reflecting on your practice is always helpful, and using a theory as a reflective lens can help you to think about the impact of the approach you took, and perhaps identify an alternative set of questions that might have been useful. This kind of reflection can also be very reassuring for us as we can see that any perceived lack of progress may well be out of our hands, and can lead to some creative ideas that we might use another time.

How, when and whether to share?

In my discussions with my theory-loving career professionals, it was very clear that they had different views about the value of sharing theories explicitly with clients. Some of this was based on the nature of the work they did – a couple of them worked with PhD students, and they found that sharing theories explicitly with their clients often worked really well. Others who worked with younger clients, or perhaps only had limited time for each one-to-one conversation, felt that sharing the theories explicitly was not practical. Even those who did like the idea of sharing theories explicitly wouldn't do it all the time.

Some of the theories are, in my view, too complex to be easily and usefully shared in a one-to-one context – I talk about the Social Cognitive Career

Theory later in the book (Chapter 9), and while it's a great theory and covers pretty much every aspect of the process, it's really complicated, and unless you are a master storyteller, you will probably lose your client's interest very early on in your description. But some of the more simple theories can be explained in just a few sentences and this can lead to some very fruitful conversations. You might need to practice a bit to make sure you find the right words to describe them – you always want to make sure that the focus is on your client and that their career issues don't get lost in the description of the theory. Sometimes it might be easier to sketch a simple diagram – that visual representation can make things easier to grasp. And you can simplify the language – I often use the more common 'confidence' rather than the more academic 'self-efficacy'. You can also reduce the theory down to one or two simple ideas. You might, for example, say to a client, 'there is a theory that shows that having some control in your work is crucial for your mental health', rather than explaining that Ryan and Deci's theory of self-determination identifies autonomy, relatedness and competence as the three basic human psychological needs (see Chapter 10). But I would urge you to give this a go. If you can find the right words, sharing the theory directly can be a powerful way to boost your client's self-awareness and self-esteem.

Which theory to choose?

We've already talked about the complexity of the world of career development theories, with different theories focusing on different things, or explaining the same thing but describing it differently. We also need to remember that there isn't always a theory that's going to work with each client or with each client's particular situation.

The key thing is to have a handful of theories that you really understand. Once you have got to know the theories reasonably well, the theories will start to choose themselves – you just listen to your clients' stories and a theory will pop into your mind. You'll find that you're not having to select a particular theory – the right theory just floats to the surface and offers itself.

Often you can see more than one relevant theory, and theories can work together in your mind to help explain the whole story. You might, for example, meet a highly capable and driven student who has what seem to be fairly tame career ambitions. There could be many explanations for this. Maybe there's nothing to unpick, and it's exactly the right choice for them – what might seem unexpected to us, might be well researched and clearly considered and might suit them perfectly. But there might be some alternative explanations, and a knowledge of theories can help you to be aware of some of the different options. Perhaps the client has had limited exposure to different occupations (Real-World Model), perhaps they are picking a job that they feel suits their gender, ethnicity and class (Circumscription and Compromise), perhaps someone they know has influenced their thinking (Community Interaction). It could be an issue with their own sense of confidence (Social Cognitive Career Theory) or perhaps they have other priorities in their life at the moment (Kaleidoscope Career Model). It could be any of these – and there are many other explanations. But armed with this knowledge, you are likely to ask some good questions to encourage your client to explore their own ideas. Your knowledge might also give you the confidence to challenge (gently and non-judgementally!) perhaps just noting to your client, that with their academic background, there would be many different routes they could take – some which might perhaps on the surface seem like more obvious options. Their response to this might help them to understand themselves better, and could help you to see more clearly what is going on, and where you could most usefully take the conversation.

Limitations

This whole book is about the value of using theory in practice. I'm a big fan of this kind of practice, and can see lots of ways in which theories can add value. But there are some important things to bear in mind. One trap I have seen myself fall into over the years is having too much faith in one particular theory. If you find yourself very drawn to a specific way of thinking, it can be tempting to see everyone's experiences through that lens – crowbarring their stories into one particular framework.

It can also be easy to jump to conclusions. As we've seen in some of the examples above, there are usually lots of possible theoretical explanations for a client's current situation, but when the first theory occurs to you, it can be easy to close your mind and assume that you've got the right one. You can then stop listening or take the conversation in a less helpful direction. Having a good understanding of a whole range of different theories is really important – this makes sure that you don't just assume that one particular theory explains things. And it's vital to remember that there are far more client stories than there are theories – it's rare that a theory will map perfectly onto a client's story. The theories are just tools to help – no theory is ever perfect.

Key takeaways

Career development theories can be useful in practice, but they won't be relevant for every conversation.

They can be used to:

- *deepen understanding and empathy*
- *give a language to articulate thoughts*
- *normalise and validate*
- *guide the conversation and*
- *support reflective practice.*

You can share the theories explicitly with clients, or just use them to help your own understanding.

Having a handful of different theories that you understand fairly well is useful so that you can pick and choose the right one, or combine them to get a fuller picture.

Chapter 5
Career theories in groups

Overview

In this chapter, we look at how to use career development theories in group settings – both in one-off, stand-alone workshops and within a programme of career education.

Introduction

For some reason, I think that we most readily imagine using theories as part of one-to-one conversations. Perhaps it's because many of the theories were developed at a time when one-to-one work dominated career practice, or perhaps it's to do with the nature of the topics that are most often covered in the two kinds of interactions: a lot of group sessions are focused on very tangible, practical transition skills like writing CVs and preparing for interviews, and maybe these aren't necessarily ones that are obviously enhanced by career development theories.

But theory-driven practice can confer the same benefits in group sessions that they do in one-to-ones – deepening understanding, boosting credibility and offering some guidance for practice. There are plenty of theories that could lend themselves particularly well to group contexts, and because you sometimes have a bit longer in a group session, there can be more time to explain some of the underpinning rationale.

Some theories lend themselves very neatly to being used as a framework to help you structure a session or a career education programme. If, for example, you want to cover some employability skills, you could take any one of the employability frameworks we look at in Chapter 12 and design your session(s) around them. If, for example, you found that you were drawn to the idea of Psychological Capital, you could identify four exercises to help your clients develop their own sense of Hope, Self-efficacy, Resilience and Optimism.

The literature (and the internet) offers plenty of relevant suggestions, and you can identify a range of activities that are client and context appropriate.

I would always recommend that you start the session with an explanation of what you are going to do and why you are going to do it. You might need to adjust your language to make sure that it resonates with your client group, but explaining that PsyCap has been shown to improve people's chances of getting a job will help to get some buy-in from your clients, and may also confirm you as the career development expert, which will do no harm.

Theories in group sessions and career education

Choose your theory
First, you need to choose your theory. In one-to-one conversations, you will often be combining theories to help you understand your client's story in the round, but with group sessions, it can work well to pick one single theory to underpin your session(s). Your choice of theory will obviously depend on what your goals are for the sessions. The different chapters in Part Two of this book are all structured around different practical issues (developing self-awareness, making career choices, etc.), so that might give you a starting point when trying to select a particular theory or planning a programme of career education.

Plan your session
The way you use the theories will obviously depend on the context in which you are working – the nature of your clients and the amount of time you've got. Once you've identified the theory or framework that you want to use, you will need to think about how it can work best in your context. Work out how much time you want to devote to each aspect of the framework, and you can start to think about practical exercises that are going to embed the learning. I've given you some ideas in the chapters that follow; the internet will give you a whole lot of other suggestions, but actually talking it through with colleagues is probably the best way to generate some suitable ideas.

Sharing the theory explicitly?
In group settings, I generally feel quite comfortable sharing the details of the theory explicitly with my clients. That holds true regardless of who they are, although I tend to adapt the language I use to the particular client group. Citing a specific theory can give you added credibility as a professional, but more importantly, it gives the session itself some credibility. Your clients will know that your choice of activities and topics is grounded in solid, thought-through, evidence-based, tried and tested ideas, and this can make clients more engaged with the session and the tasks you give them. You can spend as much or as little time on the theory as you want – perhaps just a quick

mention of the title and the name of the authors, or, if you think your clients can handle it, you could give a bit more of an introduction.

Key takeaways

Career development theories can work really well to help you structure group sessions and career education programmes.

Pick a theory that aligns well with your aims – the employability frameworks can work really well in this context.

Plan a form of words or images to explain the theory to your clients.

Identify a series of activities to address each aspect of the theory.

Part Two
Twenty-five career development theories and how to use them

Chapter 6
Theories to help explain career influences

Overview

One of the most valuable things that career professionals can do for clients is to guide them towards a better understanding of themselves. A useful starting point for this is to encourage them to think about the things, events or people that have influenced their career thinking. Here, I introduce three theories that can generate insights: Law's Community Interaction, Patton and McMahon's Systems Theory Framework and Gottfredson's theory of Circumscription and Compromise.

Introduction

In this chapter, we are focusing on theories that unpick career influences. One really important role that career professionals can play is to help clients work out where their own ideas have come from. Once clients can see what led them to this point, they are in a position to reflect on their choices – thinking about whether there have been any biases at play, and whether their awareness of the options available is sufficiently broad.

I will be introducing three approaches in this section. The first is Community Interaction, one of many theories that Bill Law left to the career community. The second is the Systems Theory Framework from Wendy Patton and Mary McMahon, which positions career choice within a whole complex system. Finally, we will look at Gottfredson's theory of Circumscription and Compromise.

Community Interaction

Introduction
This is a theory that is all about career learning, focusing on how people find out about the existence of specific occupations, how they develop their

expectations of what work is like, how people get and keep jobs and what career success is. The model focuses on communities as the major source of career learning. Communities comprise the people in our lives – our family and friends, neighbours and the people within school, university or work: the people we see and interact with regularly.

Career professionals often invite clients to reflect on where their ideas came from – this can be a good way to encourage clients to think about the reasons for their choices. But what Law suggests is that we should focus particularly on influential people: rather than asking our clients '*what gave you the idea?*', we should ask '*who gave you the idea?*'.

The theory focuses on three aspects of career learning. First, what Law describes as *coverage* – how people gain their basic knowledge of jobs, work and career options. Second, there are *processes* – how people make sense of the information. Finally, there are *influences* – which is about how other people help to shape your views about what matters.

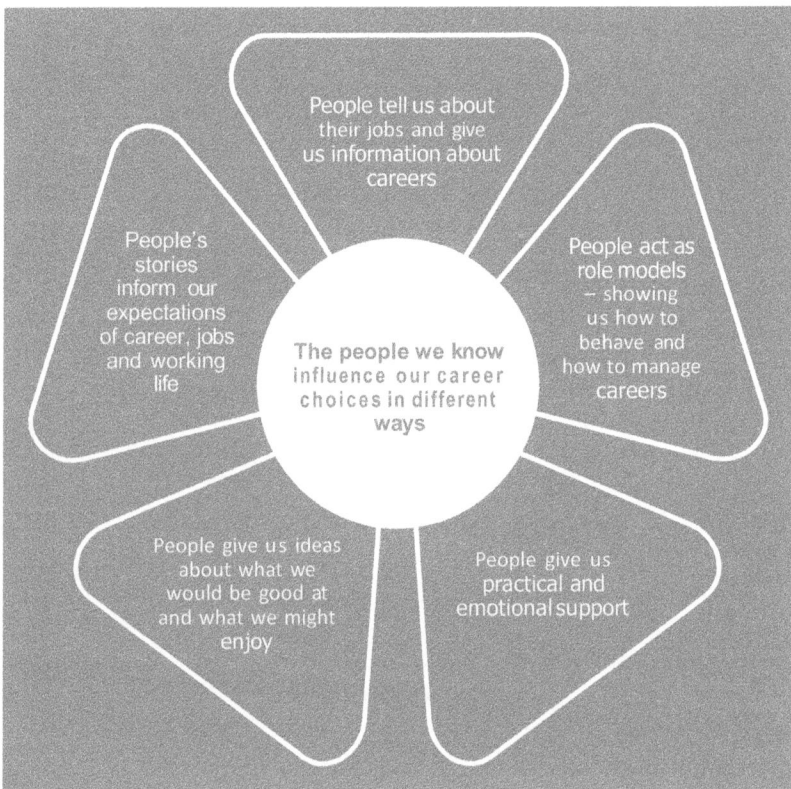

People tell us about their jobs and give us information about careers

People's stories inform our expectations of career, jobs and working life

People act as role models – showing us how to behave and how to manage careers

The people we know influence our career choices in different ways

People give us ideas about what we would be good at and what we might enjoy

People give us practical and emotional support

Figure 6.1 Law's Theory of Community Interaction.

Law identified five specific ways in which our choices and views about careers are influenced by our communities:

1) *People in our communities tell us about their jobs and give us information about careers.*

This will include our parents, whose jobs are some of the first we learn about, the jobs of people in our extended family and friends and the roles of people that we see in our daily lives, such as bus drivers, shop workers, doctors and teachers. These people give us information about the existence of these jobs and show us something about what they involve. They also give us a sense of how fulfilling the roles are and the kinds of lifestyles or social identities that are associated with different careers. These experiences also fuel assumptions about the kind of person who does particular jobs, for example, the sorts of jobs that men or women are more likely to do.

2) *People act as role models, showing us how to behave and how to manage our careers.*

We learn what constitutes professional behaviour, what people wear to work and how employees talk to clients from our own interactions with different kinds of workers. Our parents might illustrate the importance of turning up to work on time when they are rushing around in the mornings, and their stories about their conversations with their managers or colleagues give us a sense of what is expected in the workplace.

3) *People give us practical and emotional support.*

We know how valuable networking can be in career progression, and friends and family often offer us practical advice or specific opportunities. They are also the ones who will support us when things go wrong and help to rebuild our damaged egos if we are rejected from a job application.

4) *People give us ideas about what we might be good at and what we might enjoy.*

Our loved ones can sometimes see things in us that we don't see in ourselves and can often give us useful (or perhaps sometimes, not so useful) ideas about our work-related strengths. They can also offer suggestions of roles, organisations or work-related tasks that might suit us.

5) *People's stories inform our expectations of careers, work and jobs.*

We learn about the existence of work and what it means from the people around us – what a job means and how it is different from a career, whether it's a good or a bad thing, whether it's part of who a person is, or just what they do, and what career success looks like.

Community Interaction Theory in practice

Get your clients to tell stories

The best way to get people to explore their experiences is through narratives, so getting clients to tell their stories is important. Stories are how we make sense of our lives, and how we put some meaning around different events to weave them into a single, meaningful, connected journey. Asking your clients to tell their story is a useful way to get them to think about the links between various moments in the past, and the present and the future. A narrative approach can also illustrate that stories are not facts. Just asking your client to tell you their story, just using those words, hints at the idea that there is more than one interpretation of the events – more than one narrative that they could choose. This is a really useful idea to plant, as it indicates that the present and future are not fixed.

Ask your clients to reflect on their influences

A way to help clients make good decisions is to get them to reflect critically on the things that have influenced them. Ask clients to think about where their ideas and expectations have come from and who has influenced them. This can help them think about whether their sources are good enough and broad enough and whether their knowledge could be improved through additional research.

Encourage your clients to capitalise on their communities

Communities have the potential to be enormously useful. The model highlights some of the ways in which communities can have an active and positive impact on people's career learning and development. Asking clients to think about who in their community could offer them more information, support and feedback could be useful. Here are some ways you could do this:

- Ask your clients to map out some key people from their community and invite them to reflect on what each one has taught them about the nature of work.
- Get your clients to draw a map of the working people they know – if possible, ALL of the working people they know – and then ask them to list all of the occupations they do. You can then use this to get them to think about which ones they are drawn to, which they would really dislike, and to start to analyse the characteristics that appeal to them and those that don't.

- Get your client to list 20 people in their community. Ask them to take each in turn and identify one thing each person has taught them about careers and work; then ask them to identify one positive thing that each of these individuals could do to support their career planning – whether that is helpful advice, a shoulder to cry on, an introduction to someone else or a tangible opportunity. Finally, ask them to identify two or three actions they think would be most useful, and commit to putting one into practice.

NARRATIVE CAREER COACHING WITH CAREER CHANGERS

Dr Helen Cooper

I use narrative to underpin all of my practice work. When I started as a student career coach, I felt overwhelmed in my interviews with clients. They had all this information to give me, and I found it very hard to grasp, hold and make sense of all this information they would provide, particularly in their initial interviews. During my career coaching course, we came across narrative theory, and it just made sense of the career coaching practice interview for me in a number of different ways. The first is that narrative presumes that we all make sense of our lives by telling stories. And if we believe it, that means that our clients are going to come and tell us stories about their career, and our job is to help them tell their story, and then maybe re-tell it in a different way, and think about what they want in the next chapter.

Stories have a particular structure. They have a beginning, a middle and an end, and they involve a sense-making process where we start our story, then something happens in the middle, and then there's an outcome. So you have some sort of sense of temporality: something's happened in the past, and you can ask your clients about now and about what's going to happen in the future. So, I find that part of the structure really useful.

Narrative also talks about who's in the story – the key characters. That's a really nice thing to think about when somebody's talking to you and telling you about their career, who's in the story and who isn't in the story. They might talk about family, they might talk about colleagues, they might talk about people they would like to meet. You can also think about what's in their story: what do they tell you about the things that are important to them? And maybe what's missing that you need to find out about in order to make sense of the story?

Another lovely thing about narrative is that it identifies someone who is telling the story and someone who is listening: the person telling the story is the client and the person listening is us as career coaches. That reminds us that we're there to listen, and we should use all of our listening skills to try to help our clients construct a story they may never have told before. So narrative tells us about our role in relation to our client, that it's our client's story that we're looking for and our client's story that we're trying to help make sense of and perhaps to help them make sense of their own story. My job is to make sure that I've understood their story, and then I have to think about where we are going with this story – are we looking to re-author it in some way? Is it a sad story? What kind of shape does it have? And do we need to go back and investigate some of those issues? And where does the story want to go and how might we help clients get to where they want to go depending on what they've told us?

For me, narrative theory gives different ways of holding and framing all that information in what, to me, is a very useful way.

With some clients, I might ask them to do the lifeline exercise, which is where they draw almost a career story plot line. You get them to draw a little graph of their career experiences over time, and if you join the dots, this will be something like a narrative plot line – it'll have ups and downs, things that were happy and things that were sad. The lifeline exercise works really well as a way of bringing clients into that narrative method to work with them. If I have a client who likes writing, sometimes I will get them to write about where they would like to be – the story, for example, of where they would like to be.

Key takeaways

The model focuses on communities as the major influence in career learning.

Communities comprise the people in our lives – our family and friends, neighbours and the people within school or university or work.

It suggests that the question we should be asking is not 'what gave you the idea?' but 'who gave you the idea?'.

It focuses on coverage (basic knowledge), processes (how you make sense of the information) and influences.

Practitioners can encourage clients to harness their communities to give them practical and emotional support.

Using narrative approaches can help clients understand the things that have influenced them.

Systems Theory Framework of careers

Introduction

I'm pretty sure that this is the most comprehensive of all career development theories. It's described as a 'meta-theoretical framework' for career theory, meaning that it offers a framework that incorporates a host of other career theories. We've talked before about the number of different career development theories being a bit overwhelming, with dozens, probably hundreds, of theories to choose from, and theories that look at different specific aspects or domains of a career, from different angles, using slightly different words to say the same things. Patton and McMahon introduced their Systems Theory Framework (STF) as a way to help us make some sense of the array of different theories – to integrate them, showing how they work together.

It's drawn from Systems Theory, which, as the title suggests, focuses on the idea of a whole system of interdependent and interlocking factors or aspects, in which the whole is greater than the sum of the parts. Systems Theory is

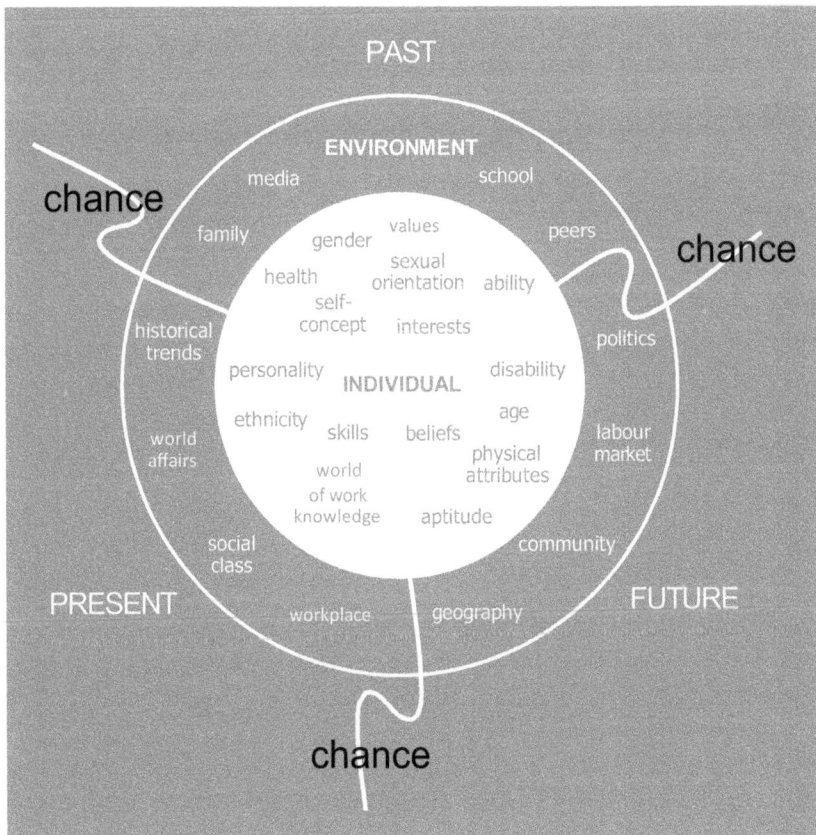

Figure 6.2 Patton and McMahon's Systems Theory Framework of career development.

transdisciplinary, meaning that it is a general idea rather than something that is domain-specific, and it has been applied very widely to a whole range of different spheres across the hard sciences, social sciences and across society.

Systems Theory Framework of career development

This framework does a really good job of incorporating all of the different factors that influence our career choices.

The model identifies individual and environmental influences. The individual influences include demographic characteristics such as gender, sexual orientation, age and ethnicity, as well as individual factors including personality, skills, values, beliefs and knowledge. Environmental factors include local influences such as family, school, peers and community, broader factors such as the media, geography, politics and world affairs, as well as historical affairs. All of these factors are then considered in terms of the individual's past, present and future, acknowledging the role of chance events. The model covers everything and as such serves an important role in illustrating how very complicated career choices are, and how much is beyond the control of the individual. I particularly like the emphasis on combining the individual and the context – highlighting both that the individual can only be understood within a context (we develop in response to everything that is around us) and that the context is only meaningful through the eyes of the individual (things have different meanings to different people).

Systems Theory Framework of career development in practice

Although the theory itself can feel both a bit overwhelming (because it's so broad) and a bit abstract (it can be hard to see what you can actually do with it), Patton and McMahon are really clear that the theory can be used to help inform practice.

It's not a theory that comes with a particular set of exercises or techniques, but instead, it is one that can be used to underpin the whole way you work with your clients.

1) *All of these factors influence each other: you can help your clients unpick their own influences and see how new information fits in.*

The authors suggest that the STF can help career professionals move away from the traditional approaches of trying to match the person and the job (such as Holland's RIASEC hexagon in Chapter 10). It can help us remember that career choices are really complex, with all sorts of factors at play, often influencing each other, and many things beyond our control. It also encourages us to conceptualise careers as meandering and bumpy rather than smooth and linear, acknowledging that career thinking moves forward unevenly as new information sheds light on existing knowledge, and people's thoughts go round in circles. One useful thing that career professionals can do is to help clients make sense of this messy thinking – helping them see how their new information might change their existing knowledge, and to integrate all the various influences and aspects of their lives and career thinking.

2) *To maintain a collaborative relationship with your client*

As career professionals, we want our relationships with our clients to be collaborative – we should be working together, each bringing different knowledge and having different roles. But in practice, in some contexts and with some clients, it's easy to fall into a more didactic role – giving information and advice. The Systems Theory Framework encourages us to think about our conversations as collaborative and exploratory – working together to unpick a problem and to look at it from a new angle. This exploratory approach helps to remind us that we don't have to have the answers.

3) *Using narrative*

We talk about narrative approaches at different points throughout this whole book. A narrative approach aligns well with the idea that reality isn't fixed or objective, and that individuals will view things individually – based on their own experiences and on their interpretation of those experiences. Narrative approaches work well with Systems Theory. Systems Theory is all about understanding how different factors influence each other. It acknowledges that this is a complicated and individual story, one that can be unpicked and understood most easily by a narrative approach that assumes there are different ways you can tell each story.

4) *For reflection*

Systems Theory can offer a valuable lens through which to understand your clients better, and you can use it as a starting point for a 'case conceptualisation' where you take one particular client and really delve deep to reflect on what has influenced them, and how these influences are interacting.

You can take your reflection one step further and start to think about yourself as a career professional being part of the system. It might be interesting to think about yourself as an influence on your client's career thinking – how could your conversation have interacted with their other influences? How else could you have steered the conversation? How would that have changed things for your client?

If you have the time, you could do some of this reflection collaboratively with your client. You could show them the diagram to aid their own reflection. You could also use it within a group session, giving each person a handout with the model on it and asking them to think about some of the factors that have influenced them.

Key takeaways

Career development is incredibly complicated.

It is influenced by a host of individual and contextual factors, and by chance events.

These factors interact with each other and are constantly changing.

It's useful to remember that career development is fluid, and that each individual person will make their own meaning from their experiences and tell their own story.

Gottfredson's theory of Circumscription and Compromise

Introduction

This is a sociological theory that focuses on the idea of occupational stereotypes and explains how these are perpetuated in our society. It is also one of the few theories that focus on children – showing how career development thinking starts at a very young age.

Critical viewpoint

Linda Gottfredson has more recently been involved in a controversial strand of research that seems to promote views that are quite at odds with my own. Because of this, I am, to be honest with you, a little bit uncomfortable about including her work in this book. But it's a useful and interesting theory, so I have decided to go ahead, with the caveat that I am in no way endorsing her position on all matters. You might want to think about how you feel about this, and make your own judgement about whether to engage with this theory.

We know that the labour market is highly segregated, and that people with different demographic characteristics (gender, ethnicity, social class) often end up in different kinds of occupations. As career professionals, this is something we are very aware of and something we try to address – we want our clients to know and feel that the full range of occupations is open to them, and we want society to benefit from occupations filled with diverse workers. Gottfredson's work helps to explain how and why people from certain groups are more likely to end up in different jobs. This is important because understanding where things go wrong can help society, career professionals and clients to redress the imbalance.

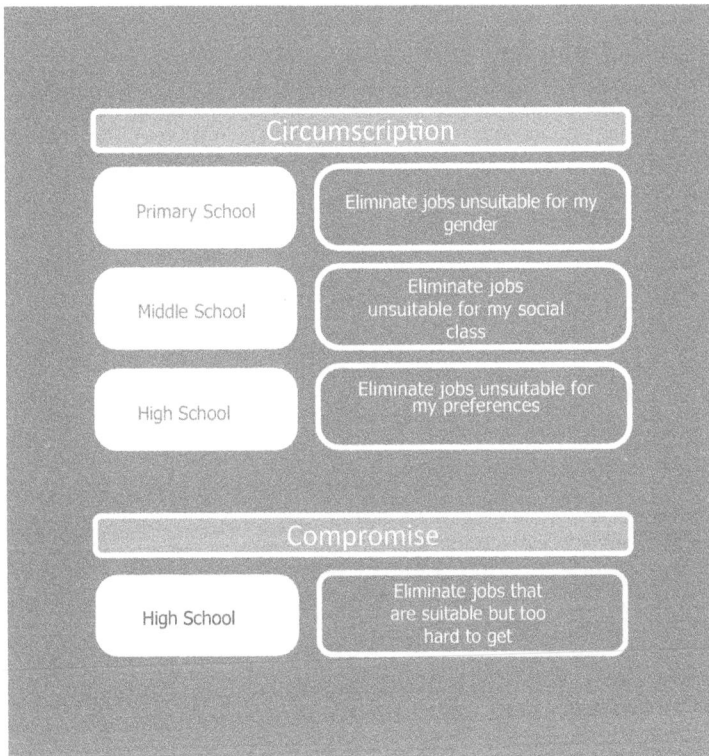

Figure 6.3 Gottfredson's theory of Circumscription and Compromise.

The theory explains the process by which children identify the sorts of jobs that they believe are suitable for people like them. It is a matching theory of sorts, showing how people choose occupations that match their self-concept. This happens in two stages: through circumscription and then through compromise.

Circumscription

Circumscription is about reducing the occupations you might consider on the basis of your demographic characteristics – limiting your sense of possible options to those that are suitable for your gender, class and ethnicity. Gottfredson describes it as the process of eliminating the options that are least suited to your self-concept. As we grow up, our self-concept becomes more nuanced and more abstract; we eliminate more and more occupations.

Early on, children's self-concept is tied up with their gender, and this first stage of circumscription tends to happen during primary school. As a child becomes aware of their own gender, and the gender of people who do various occupations, they rule out the jobs that are not suited to their gender – boys might rule out nursery nurse as a suitable occupation and girls could rule out being a surgeon. During middle school, the idea of occupational prestige starts to align with a child's understanding of their own social class, and more occupations get ruled out. The little boy who considered firefighter, lorry driver and surgeon to be suitable jobs for men when he was at primary school will make an assessment about which of those jobs aligns with his sense of his own social class, and he will eliminate those that don't suit his self-concept: a middle-class boy might rule out lorry driver and a working-class boy might eliminate surgeon from his list of suitable careers.

An important point to note is that these jobs are eliminated simply on the basis of these demographic categories – there isn't a lot of thought put into it, and children this age don't really have any understanding of what these jobs entail. They just know that people like them don't do those sorts of jobs, so they cross them off their lists.

By the time they start their teen years, a young person is starting to become aware of their own individual preferences – interests, strengths and values, and begins to understand more about the world of work. They start a more sophisticated process of seeing which roles align with their self-concept, matching the nature of the job itself to their characteristics. Here, they start to eliminate jobs that they feel they won't enjoy or that they won't be good at.

Compromise

So *circumscription* is the first stage when young people eliminate unsuitable options from their field of vision. The second stage is *compromise*, which is the process of eliminating suitable options – jobs they would like and which suit their self-concept (in terms of gender, class and preferences) but jobs that they think will be too difficult to get. Their list of remaining jobs might include some that are less compatible but more accessible. They might base this on how competitive they think the job is, how hard they are going to have to study to get the grades they need, or how easy it sounds to combine their job with their family obligations. Of course, these young people still don't know much about these jobs. They tend to rely on what are described as 'hot sources' of information – what they hear in the playground or from their parents – rather than looking to more reliable information, and are often easily put off. Gottfredson describes them as passive consumers of information rather than active seekers.

Circumscription and Compromise in practice

Start early

One important lesson from this theory is that the process of making a career choice starts early. Children will have already ruled out many jobs by the time they leave primary school, so the earlier you can start career education, the better.

Optimise learning

One of the key messages from the theory is that young people don't generally learn about occupations very well. They learn just enough about an occupation to rule it out, they trust familiar sources over and above reliable sources and their learning is quite passive – they receive the information they are given, rather than identifying what they want to know and finding it out. In large part, they do this because learning about careers is just so complicated. Anything, therefore, that we can do to simplify career learning is definitely worthwhile, making sure that all the learning opportunities we provide – in person or through websites – are age and stage appropriate.

Raise self-awareness

I mentioned above that the early decisions to rule jobs out are based on very narrow information. If you see clients who seem to have ruled out some potentially suitable jobs already, it's worth spending some time with them, helping them to reflect on the rationale for the decisions, asking what made them decide to rule a particular occupation out and what they knew about it at the time. The ideas linked with System 1 and System 2 decision-making that we cover later on in Chapter 9 might be a useful place to start.

Encourage experiences

More work-related experiences are going to be useful for anyone making a career choice. More exposure to different occupations, employers and employees is going to increase the chances that someone is exposed to a more diverse workforce – which then might stop them from concluding that particular groups of people can't do particular jobs. It's also going to build their knowledge – the more they know about a job, the more likely they are to make their choice based on a wide range of higher quality knowledge. Anything you can do to encourage more engagement will be beneficial, including work experience, job shadowing, alumni stories, career fairs and other events; and the more, the better.

Promote agency

We want young people to feel that they can make their own choices – regardless of their demographic features – and we want them to follow their dreams even if they might be challenging and ambitious. Building confidence and encouraging them to take ownership can be really important activities. Have a look at some of the ideas in Chapters 7 and 8 for some practical suggestions.

Key takeaways

Career choice starts young, when children's brains are not fully developed.

At primary school, they make very simple choices about the jobs that are open to them. They rule out:

- occupations that don't align with their gender
- occupations that don't align with their social class
- occupations that don't suit their personal preferences and
- occupations that seem too difficult.

We can help to address this by providing early, age-appropriate career interventions and ample exposure to different kinds of workers and work.

Chapter 7
Theories to help clients with their emotions

Overview

Our clients often struggle with their psychological wellbeing.

Low confidence and high anxiety can prevent clients from identifying and pursuing their career goals.

These three theories offer some ideas for supporting wellbeing.

The three theories are:

- *Self-efficacy theory*, which explains how we can help our clients feel more confident;
- *Acceptance and commitment therapy*, which offers techniques to help reduce the impact of negative thoughts and feelings; and
- *The PERMA model of wellbeing*, which explains the five pillars of happiness.

Introduction

I'm sure you will all recognise the part that negative emotions can play in preventing clients from reaching their potential. Two of the most common negative emotions that we see in our clients are anxiety and low confidence, and both of these have been shown to have a negative impact on career development. One way they hold us back is through avoidance tactics. In order to avoid experiencing these negative emotions, we tend to avoid actions that risk making us feel bad: we might not go along to a useful networking event because we imagine it will make us feel awkward, or we decide not to apply for a job because of fear of rejection. The result is that when we are feeling anxious and unconfident, we find it more difficult to identify, pursue and reach our career goals.

It is also sadly clear that negative emotions are becoming more and more common in our clients. The Covid pandemic seems to have exacerbated an already worrying trend in our young people's mental ill-health, and we are seeing more and more young people who are suffering from low self-confidence and anxiety.

> ### 💡 Practice tip
>
> When working with emotions, it's important that we think about our boundaries. Most career professionals are not trained counsellors, and we need to be mindful that we are not skilled or resourced to support severe levels of mental ill-health. If you feel that your client's psychological state is preventing them from moving forward or living the life they want to live, it may be useful to have a discussion with them about seeking professional counselling. Having said that, many clients can benefit from a boost to their wellbeing, so having some techniques at your disposal that can help may have a positive knock-on impact on your clients' ability to make career choices, on their motivation and their chances of career success.

Having a greater understanding of what might lie behind some of these negative feelings can help us to assist our clients in understanding themselves a little better and perhaps moving forward more positively.

There are three theories I want to introduce in this chapter. The first is Bandura's theory of self-efficacy, which focuses on confidence; secondly, Acceptance and Commitment Therapy, which helps people manage the impact their anxiety has; and finally, we will look at Seligman's PERMA model of wellbeing from positive psychology, which identifies five key factors that contribute to psychological wellbeing.

Self-efficacy theory

Introduction

Self-efficacy seems to come up a lot across career development research. Self-efficacy is *context-specific confidence*; it is the degree to which a person feels confident about their ability to perform a specific action or succeed in a particular context. Your confidence in your ability to succeed at a job interview could be called 'job interview self-efficacy', your confidence in your ability to do well in an exam would be your 'exam self-efficacy' and, one that comes up a lot in the literature, your confidence in your ability to make a career choice is described as your 'career decision-making self-efficacy'. Self-efficacy has been shown to have a huge impact on career outcomes. It helps people make good choices, get jobs and then perform well at work. Self-efficacy even seems to have more of an impact than actual ability.

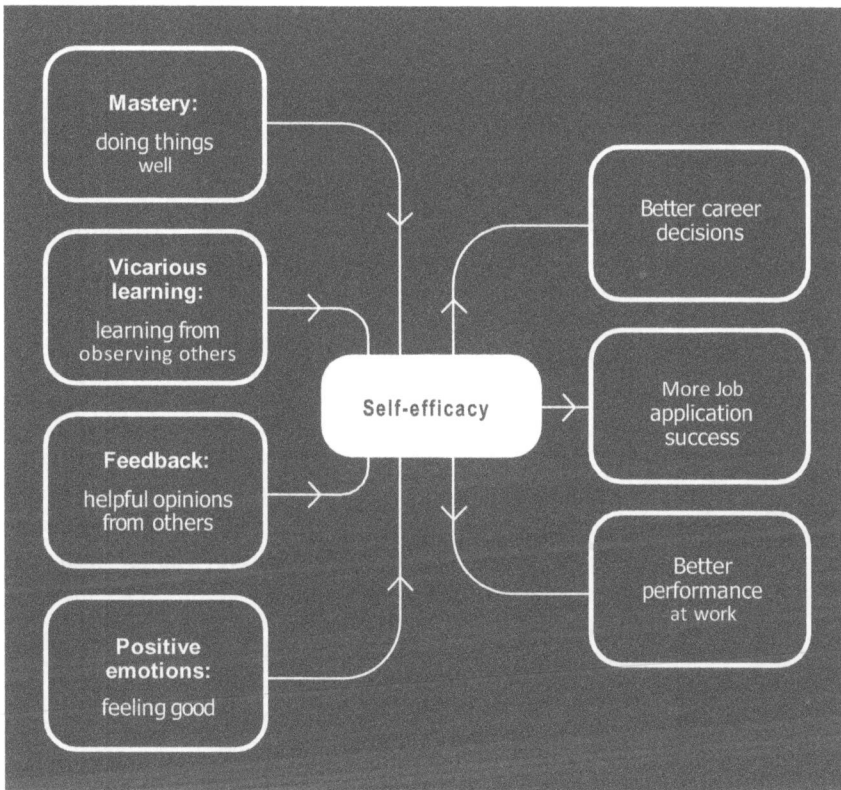

Figure 7.1 Bandura's theory of self-efficacy.

One particular strand of research into self-efficacy focuses on gender. Back in the 1980s, Betz and Taylor in the US identified that much of the reason for women and men's different career paths lay in their different levels of self-efficacy. This has been shown widely in research that explores the reasons for women's under-representation in STEM areas (science, technology, engineering and maths), which consistently finds that women don't feel as confident in their STEM abilities as their male counterparts, and this has a significant impact on their choices.

This isn't the only time we will come across the concept of self-efficacy within this book. Self-efficacy is at the core of Lent et al.'s Social Cognitive Career Theory in Chapter 9. We will also will come across it later on when we look at Savickas and Porfeli's model of Career AdaptAbilities in Chapter 8. But Bandura, back in the 1970s, was the real pioneer in this field, unpicking what self-efficacy is and how we develop it.

Self-efficacy beliefs have an impact because they change the way we look at the challenges we are facing. If self-efficacy is high, we see challenges in a positive way – as things we can overcome, rather than as pointless activities to be avoided. High levels of self-efficacy also mean that we believe that we have more control over outcomes. We see setbacks as temporary things that are the result of insufficient effort and therefore feel that it will be worthwhile to put additional effort into working towards our goals. People with high self-efficacy then are more likely to set themselves more ambitious goals, are more likely to work harder to achieve them, and are more resilient in the face of setbacks.

Bandura describes four sources of self-efficacy:

1) *Mastery experiences.* The most effective way to build self-efficacy is to do something well. If you engage in an activity and your efforts are successful (i.e. if you 'master' it), then your belief in your own ability will grow. These experiences of personal success are the best route to building confidence, and the harder the task you master, the more impact it will have on your confidence.

2) *Vicarious learning.* This means learning through watching others. If you see someone else succeeding in a particular task, it gives you the opportunity to work out how they did it and identify the specific steps that led to their success. This analysis not only gives you a blueprint for your own actions but can make you believe that success is possible: if someone else can do it, then maybe, so can you. This works particularly well if the person is someone similar to you or someone you can easily relate to.

3) *Feedback.* Receiving specific feedback about your abilities in a relevant activity can make you feel more confident about your chances. If someone else tells you that they believe in you, then you are much more likely to believe in yourself. Even if the feedback is somewhat critical, you will at least be in a position to know what you need to work on, and that can also make you believe that you can succeed.

4) *Positive emotions.* Just feeling positive – happy, engaged, proud or joyful – can help you to feel more confident.

For self-efficacy to have the most impact it needs to be grounded in reality. People who are 'over-efficacious' (i.e. who believe that they are significantly better than they actually are) often don't perform well because they don't feel the need to prepare or work hard, and may therefore be less likely to achieve. Although some of our clients might be a little overconfident, it's much more common to see people whose confidence needs building.

Self-efficacy in practice
To underpin your approach to your clients

Almost every client we see will benefit from a confidence boost, so just keeping the four sources of self-efficacy in mind is useful. If you can remember how important it is for choosing and getting a job, and that many of our clients are likely to have low levels of self-efficacy, then having the four sources at the forefront of your mind can help you identify and capitalise on any opportunity to boost your clients' confidence.

Specific exercises

In addition, there are specific ideas that you might want to consider when dealing with clients whose self-confidence clearly needs some extra work.

1) *Mastery*: This is the most powerful route to increasing self-efficacy, so if you can see a chance to allow your clients to get some practice, it can really make a difference.

   ✔ If you are hoping to boost your client's chances of success in a job application, then there are several activities that can work – whether that is a mock interview, a run-through of a presentation or a practice psychometric test.

   ✔ If the thing they need to try is beyond the scope of a career intervention, you could share this aspect of the theory explicitly with them – explaining that the best way to increase confidence is to actually have a go at something, and then the two of you together could brainstorm ideas.

2) *Vicarious learning*: Learning from others can be a useful approach to both show clients how to do something and to make them believe that they can succeed. How you manage this best will depend on the context in which you are working.

   ✔ If you are working in a group setting, you can use one group member's success to show others how things can be done. This may work best with a smaller group, where some psychological safety has already been established and the group can relate to each other and will want to celebrate others' successes.

   ✔ In larger, more formal contexts, you could bring in speakers to talk about their own journeys. For the purpose of vicarious learning, these speakers should be people your clients can relate to. If you are working in a school or college, they could be ex-students just one or two years out, whose paths might be similar to those your clients are considering. High achievers can be inspirational figures, but don't usually do much for clients' own self-efficacy as people can feel they could never match up to these exceptional characters.

✔ Another approach is to develop your own bank of case studies. Collect stories of people in all sorts of situations overcoming challenges and meeting their goals. You can use these in one-to-ones to show your clients that success is possible for people just like them.

3) *Feedback*: Use any opportunity to give your clients positive feedback.

✔ When you are looking at their CV, find as many positives as you can and share them explicitly with your client.

✔ When hearing your client's stories, identify the skills and resources they have demonstrated and spend some time discussing their strengths.

✔ If you are working with groups, you could also encourage positive feedback within the group – identifying opportunities for clients to give positive feedback to each other.

4) *Positive emotions*: It's very difficult to feel confident about your own chances of success when you are in a negative mood. Any techniques that you can use to boost your clients' general mood can make a difference, and later in the chapter I will cover Seligman's PERMA model, which gives a number of specific ideas for boosting emotions.

Key takeaways

Self-efficacy is a context-specific measure of confidence – how confident someone feels about succeeding in doing one particular task, for example, applying for a job or getting a good mark in an exam.

Self-efficacy has a huge impact on people's chances of choosing and getting a job, and on their ability to perform well.

Bandura has identified specific things that can help to boost self-efficacy:

● *Mastery experiences*: Offer your client opportunities to try difficult tasks out in a safe space.

● *Vicarious learning*: Let your clients learn from each other's successes.

● *Positive feedback*: Look for opportunities to give (authentic) positive feedback.

Acceptance and commitment therapy

Introduction

Acceptance and commitment therapy, known as ACT (pronounced 'act' – as one word), is one of a number of behavioural analysis approaches that have become very popular over the last few decades. These approaches all acknowledge the links between thoughts, emotions and behaviour, and give ideas to help people make positive changes.

The most common of these approaches, and one that you might have come across before, is cognitive behavioural therapy (CBT). This acknowledges that emotions and behaviours are difficult to change and offers techniques to help people change their thinking – to identify faulty or unhelpful patterns of thinking and then to develop new, more helpful thinking habits. CBT has been shown to work well, but it's not easy – it relies on developing habits and requires a lot of dedicated practice.

In contrast, ACT understands that sometimes changing our thoughts is just too hard. Instead, ACT tries to work on the impact that the negative thoughts have. ACT is all about finding ways that we can to make our peace with (accept) the thoughts but try to make sure that they don't stop us from living the lives we want to live – committing to values-driven action. It's a sort of 'feel the fear and do it anyway' approach.

ACT was originally developed for use with clinical populations – with people really struggling with depression or anxiety. More recently, it's been shown to be effective in dealing with workplace stress, and there have been a few research papers published showing its value in a career context. It lends itself really well to career practice – we so often see people who are suffering from career anxiety, and it's great to be able to offer them some techniques that might help.

The goal of ACT is to equip people with what the authors call *psychological flexibility* – the ability to make choices about what to think about and how to think about it. This psychological flexibility enables people to stop ruminating on the past and to stop worrying about the future, focusing instead on doing what they need in order to live the life they want to live.

ACT works towards psychological flexibility by encouraging people to do three things:

- to be aware;
- to open up; and
- to do what matters.

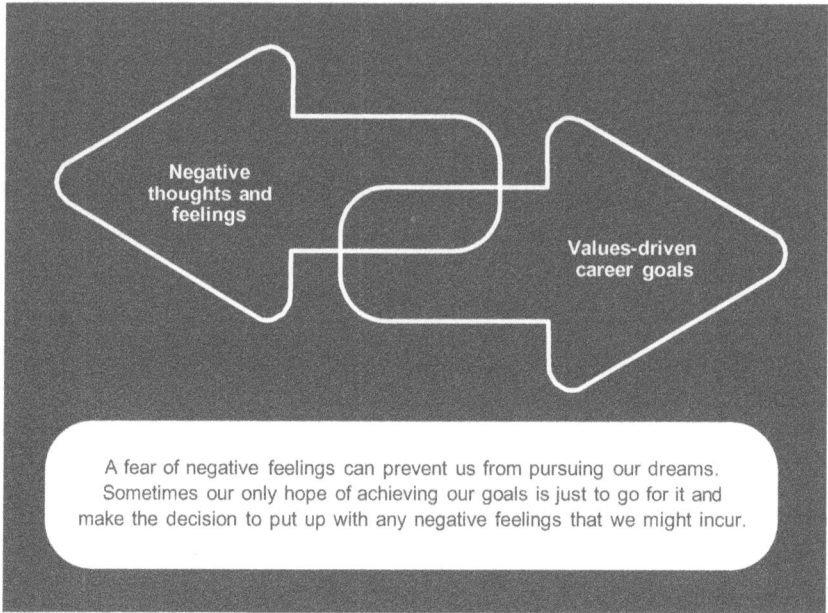

Negative thoughts and feelings

Values-driven career goals

A fear of negative feelings can prevent us from pursuing our dreams. Sometimes our only hope of achieving our goals is just to go for it and make the decision to put up with any negative feelings that we might incur.

Figure 7.2 Acceptance and commitment therapy.

We become *aware* by noticing what is going on inside us – observing the negative and unhelpful thoughts and feelings and noticing the impact that they have on us both internally – how we feel, and externally – how we behave.

When we *open up*, we accept negative thoughts, understand them for what they are – thoughts, not realities, and we decide – we make a choice, to put up with them in order to pursue our goals.

Doing what matters entails first identifying our values and then deciding to commit to action.

ACT in practice
ACT can be useful when working with clients whose anxiety seems to be preventing them from pursuing their career goals.

Share the message explicitly
If you are working with a client whose fears are stopping them from putting their plans into action, it can be useful to share the overall ACT message. Ask them the question: what negative feelings are you prepared to put up with, in order to pursue your goals? This can lead to an enlightening conversation in which clients realise that they do have a choice – their own behaviour doesn't

need to be at the mercy of their emotions and thoughts; it can be within their control.

Specific exercises
Mindfulness to help clients to be aware

Mindfulness can help people become more aware as they focus on the present moment. Mindfulness is a form of secular meditation that trains people to be present in the moment and can help them stop ruminating on the past or worrying about the future. There are hundreds of guided meditations that you can find online, but a really simple one involves inviting your client to close their eyes and just focus on their breathing. Encourage them to think about the breath going in and to notice their lungs filling up with air, and then to focus on the breath as it goes out and their chest goes down. You can suggest they count 10 or 20 breaths in this way and then ask them to reflect on how it has made them feel.

Passengers on the bus to help clients to open up

An exercise to help people accept their negative thoughts is the *Passengers on the Bus* metaphor, which reinforces the idea that people can make choices about their actions and that sometimes putting up with negative or unhelpful thoughts and feelings can be worth it. The metaphor runs along these lines:

> *Imagine that you are driving a bus. This bus represents your life or your career, and as the bus driver, you are completely in charge of the destination, the route and the speed. But on the bus are some disruptive, unruly passengers. These represent your unhelpful or negative thoughts and feelings. The passengers are hurling abuse at you, trying to force you to slow down, speed up, or turn left, or stop altogether. But you have a choice. Your hands are on the wheel, and your feet are on the pedals, and you can choose what you do. You can't stop the passengers from shouting or change what they are saying. But you can decide how to respond. You could listen to the passengers and do what they say: slow down, speed up or turn left or stop. Or you could continue on your journey. You will have to put up with the passengers' shouting – you aren't going to stop them, but you will end up at your chosen destination.*

The Retirement Party to help people to do what matters

An approach to support doing what matters is the Retirement Party exercise, which helps people identify their values. In this exercise, people are invited to think ahead into the future and imagine their own retirement party. They are asked to write the speech that they would like their boss to give in their honour – highlighting the kinds of achievements they might have made throughout their working lives, the strengths they could have shown and the impact that they might have made during their careers. This exercise helps people identify their values and work out what a values-driven career could look like for them.

ACT WITH CAREER CHANGERS

Ross McIntosh

I've developed my expertise in ACT because I see its utility in so many different areas of coaching and organisational work. It forms the foundation of everything that I do. In this career-change example, I used questions based on ACT to really help a client explore her current situation. I was working with someone who was in the corporate world in professional services. She had advanced rapidly. She was a bit of a rising star, very intelligent, very hard-working, and she was set to be the youngest partner in the firm. But she was despondent and miserable.

This client came to me because she had an inkling that she was in the wrong career, the wrong job. In fact, it was more than an inkling. She was really fed up, and first of all, using ACT principles, it was just about giving her some space to unpack everything and to talk about what matters to her in her career – her work-related values. This client talked a lot about service to others, supporting people to be healthy and well in the workplace, and it became really clear that these values weren't really aligned with her current role and would probably be even less relevant if she became a partner.

So we then started to explore what would be a good, positive next step – one that would be aligned with her values. She worked out that what she needed to do next was to speak to her boss about her frustrations. She was pretty clear that this is what she needed to do. But then this client started to talk about all sorts of unhelpful ideas – you know how our minds can produce all sorts of unhelpful stuff that gets in the way of us doing the things we actually want to do. A whole host of things was showing up for her: *my boss is going to persuade me to stay; they're gonna talk about my glittering future, and why would I throw away the prospect of all this future money?*

And it was then really that we started to unpack that her whole career had been about pleasing other people and doing what she thought she *should* do because of pressure, enthusiasm and pride from her family, who were so proud of her progress, her career and her success. She said that she felt she was moving so fast through life that she had no time to stop and even look at the flowers, let alone smell them. That just seemed so sad, but such an important revelation.

And then we were able to map out her next steps. We mapped out an exploration, which allowed her to go back to her further studies, to explore her interest and curiosity about mental health, but also to start exploring other areas of physical health and maybe even take a qualification in something different. So we mapped out some small steps to allow her to really set a vision for her future and using ACT really allowed her to think about what's important and who's important and to identify some small steps towards that. But also getting all that stuff out about *what will people think? I'm throwing away a glittering career. I could make lots of money,* all of that and to see that it really wasn't aligned with what was really fundamentally deep down, important to her. And I think that is what made the difference.

🔒 Key takeaways

Negative and unhelpful thoughts and feelings can stop us from making good choices.

Sometimes it is possible to make ourselves stop thinking the thoughts, but sometimes this is too difficult.

But we can make the choice to take a risk, or to put up with the negative feelings in order to pursue our goals.

For example, applying for a job will always entail the risk of rejection.

We can either protect ourselves from the rejection and choose not to apply, or we can decide that we will go for the job and risk rejection.

In other words, we should feel the fear and do it anyway.

Seligman's PERMA model of wellbeing

Introduction

Back in 2000, Seligman and his colleague Csikszentmihalyi (pronounced Chick-sent-me-high) proposed a whole new approach to psychology. Traditionally, psychology had been focused on those who were struggling, and its goal was to find ways to help these people cope. Seligman and Csikszentmihalyi wanted to broaden the scope of psychology. They suggested that alongside this traditional focus, there was a place for a discipline that focused on people who were coping okay with life, and looked for ways to help them thrive and flourish. They described this as Positive Psychology. Positive psychologists have conducted a lot of large-scale research over the last two decades looking at the notion of psychological wellbeing, and have identified five key pillars of wellbeing, which they describe through the PERMA model.

The PERMA model

The five pillars are:

- **P**ositive emotions;
- **E**ngagement;
- **R**elationships;
- **M**eaning; and
- **A**ccomplishments.

Each of these five pillars will boost wellbeing both across life broadly and specifically at work, enhancing work-related wellbeing and increasing job satisfaction. On top of this, wellbeing can improve our ability to make good career decisions, our chances of getting a job and our ability to bounce back if things go wrong.

Positive emotions are as straightforward as they sound. It's just about feeling happy and positive. In a work context, you might get this from a lovely view out of your window, a nice lunch or a compliment from a customer.

Engagement is a measure of how focused you are – how 'into' your work you are. There are some personality types who, by their nature, are more likely to get involved in their work than others, but for all of us, engagement is more likely if we genuinely care about the work we do.

Relationships come up in almost every taxonomy or scale about wellbeing. They are so important. In a work context, we need to be able to develop positive relationships with colleagues, customers and clients, and have people in our work lives that we feel connected to – whether through working towards a common goal, sharing values or just having some good-natured office banter.

Meaning is increasingly emerging in the literature as key to a positive life. A meaningful job is one that you feel matters – one that aligns with your own values, in which you feel you are genuinely making a difference, and one that connects you to something bigger than yourself – whether that's a team or organisation that you feel part of, or a cause or community beyond your office.

Accomplishment is about feeling that you are achieving something. Whether that is completing a project, mastering a new skill, producing something tangible or getting some meaningful positive feedback, feeling that you are actually getting somewhere and have something to show for your efforts is important.

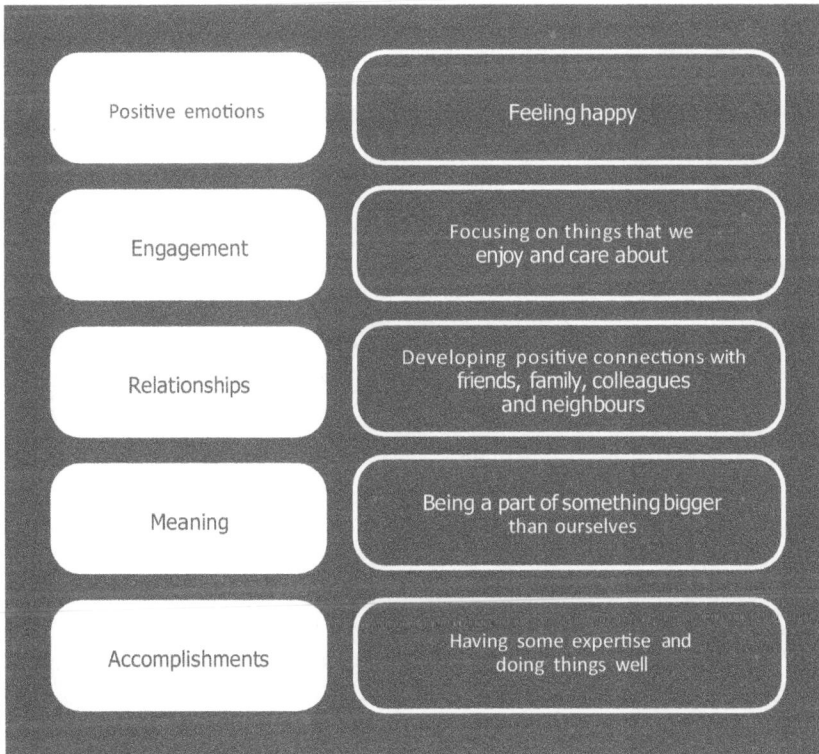

Positive emotions	Feeling happy
Engagement	Focusing on things that we enjoy and care about
Relationships	Developing positive connections with friends, family, colleagues and neighbours
Meaning	Being a part of something bigger than ourselves
Accomplishments	Having some expertise and doing things well

Figure 7.3 Seligman's PERMA model of wellbeing.

The PERMA model in practice

As a way to develop understanding. Sharing the PERMA model explicitly with clients can sometimes help them understand why things aren't going well for them at work. If your client mentions problems with one or two of these five pillars when they are telling their story, you might want to share the model explicitly with them, explaining (briefly) that these five things are all needed for psychological wellbeing. Knowing that there is a reason for their struggles – that their experience is 'a thing' – can be really validating and can help people understand, accept and forgive themselves.

To identify positive strategies. The model can be used as a starting point for ideas to improve psychological wellbeing. With some clients, you might want to share the model explicitly and then collaboratively brainstorm ideas to improve things. (What could you do to develop better relationships with colleagues? How could you find more meaning within your job?) Alternatively, you could suggest some of the positive psychology techniques for boosting wellbeing. Here are a few examples that have been shown to have a significant and lasting impact on wellbeing, but you can find many more online.

- Write a gratitude letter: Ask your client to write a letter to someone who has influenced them, explaining the impact of their support. They don't need to send the letter, but the process of thinking about how someone has helped them has been shown to boost wellbeing.

- Random acts of kindness: Evidence shows that performing a random act of kindness for a stranger has a positive impact. Ask your client to initiate one act of kindness each day – such as holding a door for someone, paying a compliment to a stranger or giving some money to someone in need.

- Three good things: Every evening on their way home from work, ask your client to reflect on the day and identify three good things that have happened to them. These don't need to be particularly significant – a nice chat with a colleague, a productive meeting or even a tasty sandwich lunch would all work nicely. The value in this exercise is in making it a habit. If you know that you are going to have to come up with three positives at the end of every day, you start to think about your daily activities through a more positive lens.

Key takeaways

Psychological wellbeing makes us enjoy work and life more, makes us more resilient and improves our chances of thriving at work.

The PERMA model identifies five pillars of wellbeing, and research shows that having all five in our lives improves mental health.

The five pillars are: Positive emotions, Engagement, Relationships, Meaning and Accomplishment.

Knowing about the five pillars can help us identify useful strategies for our clients.

Chapter 8
Theories to help clients take ownership of their career planning

Overview

Clients often struggle to take ownership of their own career planning –
sometimes because it can seem too daunting and sometimes because they
don't understand what they need to do.

In this section I introduce three theories that can help to give clients agency
over their own career development:

- *Planned Happenstance* is a descriptive model that can reassure clients
  who are struggling with their career planning, and offers them some
  ideas to help them to capitalise on chance opportunities.
- *Career Construction Theory* introduces the idea of designing your own
  life, emphasising the integration of life and career, and acknowledging
  the fluid nature of career paths.
- *Career AdaptAbilities* builds on one of the key ideas in Career
  Construction Theory and offers the *Four Cs* model of characteristics
  needed to cope with the modern world of work: Concern, Control,
  Confidence and Curiosity.

Introduction

One common challenge we face as practitioners is how to help clients who
aren't taking ownership of their own career development – those who want
us to tell them what to do, or those who perhaps expect fate to step in and
sort things out for them. There can be all sorts of reasons for this lack of
ownership. A common reason is low confidence, but we also see clients who
simply don't know how career planning works, and who lack agency because
they haven't realised that this is something they need to do. Some clients
perhaps are struggling because they haven't really had to own any decision

before, and are just assuming that it's your job to tell them what to do, or perhaps they just find it all rather scary and would rather someone else took control so that if it were to go wrong, they would have someone else to blame. Whatever the reason, we know that they are never going to make their best choices if they don't own the process and the career decision.

I will be introducing three theories in this section. The first is Planned Happenstance, which can help clients to see that career planning may not be as daunting as they fear; secondly I will introduce Savickas' idea of Career Construction; and finally, the Career AdaptAbilities model, which can help people to develop the skills or attitudes they need for career planning.

Planned Happenstance

Introduction

This is one of the most popular and well-used career theories. It is a descriptive theory, meaning that it literally describes how people's careers actually unfold. This differs from many of the theories we cover in this book which are prescriptive theories – those that give advice on what people should be doing – prescribing how they can do it better. Of course, as career professionals, we want to help our clients do things better – that is the whole point of our jobs. But the advice we give needs to be relatable – it will be much easier for our clients to put new strategies into practice if the approach builds on their natural or instinctive approaches rather than try to replace them altogether. And that's where the magic of Planned Happenstance lies.

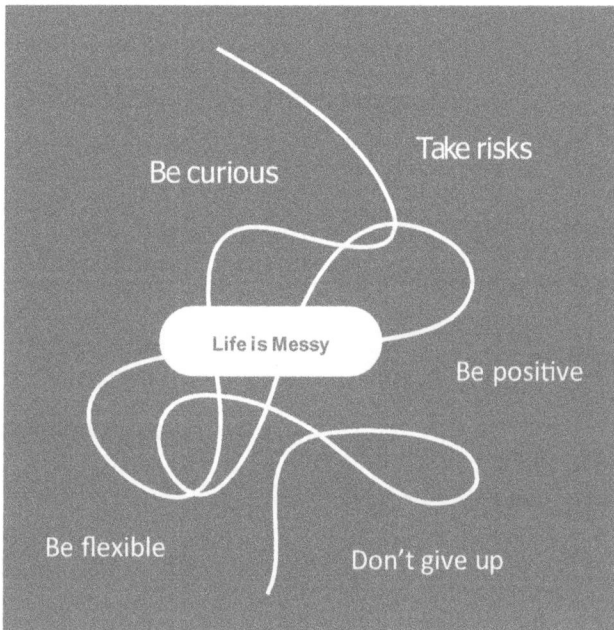

Figure 8.1 Mitchell et al.'s theory of Planned Happenstance.

The starting point of Planned Happenstance is the understanding that most people's career paths are a bit haphazard. Traditional advice advocates clear career goals and five-year plans, but in reality, very few of us are that clear sighted and even those who have specific career goals can find themselves facing unexpected decisions as life, as we know, doesn't always go to plan.

The theory of Planned Happenstance acknowledges the messiness of our lives and careers and the huge impact and potential that can come from chance opportunities. But it also buys into the idea that you can make your own luck – you can make choices about what you look for, what you see and how you respond to what comes your way.

The key message of the theory is that we should make sure that we look out for chance opportunities and then capitalize on them. This mindset will then allow us to make the most of whatever life throws at us. It can also make us more resilient. It shows that the world is not predictable, and that if you don't end up exactly where you planned to be, it isn't necessarily a problem, embracing the principle that when one door closes another one opens.

Five Planned Happenstance principles

The authors have identified five Planned Happenstance principles. They suggest that we should try to live our lives according to them, and this will help us to be more open to opportunities and better able to respond to those that cross our paths.

Be curious. The more you open your mind the more chances will come your way. Be interested in finding out about different careers, different approaches, different ideas and this might lead to more ideas and opportunities.

Be flexible. Goals and plans can be useful – they can make us more motivated and resilient – but if we stick to them too rigidly, they can start to limit us. It's great to have some sense of direction, but it's important to recognize that there is no single perfect job, and certainly not only one way to get to it. If opportunities come your way, you need to be able to change your mindset and take advantage of them, even if it takes you away from your set course.

Take risks. Things won't always work out, but that's okay – that's just how life is. If you decide to take a risk, there is chance that things will go wrong. But there is also a chance that they will go well, and if you don't try, you will never know.

Be positive. Every opportunity will teach you something. Even the worst job, the most humiliating job interview, the most excruciating networking opportunity all push us forward, allowing us to understand a bit more about ourselves and the world.

Don't give up. For most of us, things won't come easily. We have to work and try and fail and then work and try again. To reap the rewards you want, you need to stick with it, and try to enjoy the journey.

Planned Happenstance in practice

1) To reassure clients. This can be a good theory to share explicitly with clients whose careers have not gone quite to plan – it can help to normalise and validate the choices they have made, getting them to see that a seemingly haphazard or incoherent career path is very natural, and does not indicate that anything has gone wrong or that they have failed in any way.

2) To help clients to be more flexible. It can also be useful to share with clients who seem quite rigid in their approach to career planning – either unhelpfully fixed on a particular goal, or anxious about trying to find the 'right' career path.

3) To increase our empathy as practitioners. The theory is a helpful reminder for practitioners that being undecided is not necessarily a problem.

4) To structure career education. The five principles needed to spot, identify and capitalise on chance opportunities can be used to help structure career education.

PLANNED HAPPENSTANCE WITH YEAR ELEVENS

Anna Brandon

Since Covid I've really noticed something with the year elevens. I would always ask them about what they do in their spare time, their activities, hobbies, interests, etc. And I noticed that so many of them started telling me about the hobbies that they *used* to do: I used to play tennis or go gymnastics club or be part of an orchestra or go to dance, and then they would always say 'and then there was Covid'. They stopped all these things because of Covid and getting back into them has been really tricky for them.

So that's when I bring in the theory of Planned Happenstance and talk about the opportunities that they might have by doing activities, meeting people, opening up different experiences. Then occasionally I meet one or two that say, oh yeah, I used to go to dance and then I stopped because of Covid, but I've just gone back to it now. And those are the ones I really celebrate because I'm so impressed with that kind of resilience that has enabled them to go back to something that they've left for a couple of years and recognise what it gave them in terms of not just the career opportunities, but all those mental and physical health benefits of engaging in extracurricular activities.

I am explicit sometimes about the theory because I think then it isn't just me giving praise or saying, why don't you try this? There's an actual theory that suggests this. It just gives it that bit of credibility I think and makes them think, oh actually, okay, there's someone out there, an academic that thinks this is going to make a difference. There's a theory which makes you think that there really could be a positive outcome by doing this particular thing that this careers adviser is suggesting.

Key takeaways

It can be easy to think that having a fixed career plan that we stick to rigidly is a good thing.

In truth, careers are generally very messy.

Life is full of unexpected opportunities which we only see if we are looking and which we can only capitalise on if we are prepared to be flexible and take risks.

Career Construction Theory

Introduction

Career Construction Theory is the brainchild of Mark Savickas, one of the big names in career academia over the last generation. Career Construction is all about agency – the belief that you have some control and power over your own life and future. Career Construction Theory holds that people construct their own careers and that rather than slotting into any kind of pre-planned, pre-destined, tried and tested career path, people can and should take control and design their own careers.

Savickas aims to combine the best of three different groups of career theories, taking some ideas from matching theories, some from the developmental approaches and some from narrative theories. Career Construction suggests that people should think about what kinds of jobs they are suited to

71

(matching), how people learn to cope with the challenges of careers and work (developmental) and why people make the choices they do – how they tell their stories (narrative). He describes Career Construction as a theory that is fit for the modern world, with all of its complexities and shape-shifting. It's a theory that can account for the whole career lifespan, and encourages people to keep developing, reflecting, adjusting and striving throughout their whole careers, making choices that allow them to have a lifetime of meaningful career fulfilment.

Life themes

At the heart of Career Construction Theory is the idea that careers are all about what matters: what matters to you, and how your choices matter to other people. It's about the meaning that people put on their experiences – the way they interpret what has happened to them, and the meaning that they want to find in their lives and careers. Career Construction Theory is very linked to narrative approaches to counselling – an approach that sees a person's career as a story that can be told and re-told in different ways at different times. It's notable that Savickas very much talks about 'life' themes, and indeed, one of his other big ideas is called Life Design. In both of these, he is making the point that you can't really separate *career* and *life*.

Vocational personality

This aspect of Career Construction Theory builds on the more traditional kind of matching approaches. It focuses on what an individual might have to offer an employer, and how they might look for a job where those attributes are useful. Your *vocational personality* includes things like your career interests, strengths, needs and values. This mirrors the traditional matching approaches, such as Holland's RIASEC model, which we cover in Chapter 10, but here, Career Construction Theory conceptualises these attributes and their relationship with work slightly differently. Rather than a set of fixed characteristics that need to fit neatly with a rigid work role, Career Construction Theory sees these characteristics as far more flexible – as social constructs rather than tangible attributes – our interpretations of ourselves, or stories that we tell ourselves, rather than facts. In terms of Career Construction, these characteristics are a good starting point for thinking about how we want to see ourselves, who we want to become and how we can adapt both our selves and our jobs to mould to each other.

Career Adaptability

Building on that idea of being able to adapt, Career Adaptability is the third key concept within Career Construction Theory. The assumption is that both individuals and jobs need to adapt – both to each other and to the ever-shifting environment, re-inventing themselves all the time to keep relevant

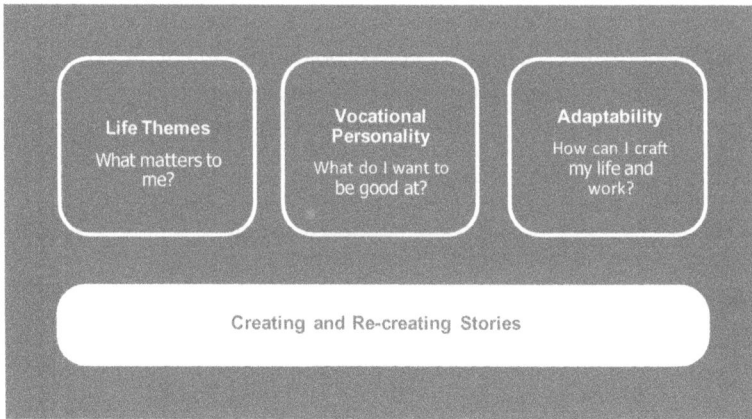

Figure 8.2 Savickas' Career Construction Theory.

and to face the future. I'll go on to talk about this idea in more detail in part three of this chapter.

Critical perspective

Savickas is very much a psychologist. This means that his starting point for thinking about career development is the individual – he focuses on what is going on within the individual and what they can do themselves to make any changes. Other career theorists come from a more sociological perspective – they are more likely to start thinking about the context – focusing on what impact the environment in which the person is operating, will have on their careers. Savickas in this theory focuses on agency – on the importance of feeling some sense of ownership over your own career choices. The research does show that this makes a big difference, so it is definitely important for us to engage with this – these sorts of ideas and exercises can really help our clients. But Savickas' critics argue that he goes a bit far down this line, almost ignoring the impact of environmental factors and assuming that everyone has an equal chance to excel.

Career Construction Theory in practice

To apply Career Construction Theory in career counselling, Savickas developed the *Career Style Interview*. This is a series of interesting and insightful questions to help your clients to tell, understand and reflect on their own stories. Savickas suggests that these questions allow people to identify their 'life themes' and they can be valuable to think about any common threads running through your clients' answers.

The full Career Style Interview has nine quite meaty questions. Asking all of the questions is time-consuming and probably too much for the context in which most of us practice, but these are the ones that I find lead to the most insightful conversations, and asking even one or two can lead to some fruitful discussions.

Career Style Interview (adapted from Savickas)

1. Who do you admire? OR Who did you admire when you were growing up?
   a. In what ways are you similar or different from them?
   b. What advice would they give you?
   c. How would your life / career be different if you were to live your life more like them?
2. What are your favourite TV shows / podcasts / social media influencers?
   a. What do you like about them?
3. What is your all-time favourite story?
   a. Who is your favourite character – why do you like them and in what ways are you similar to or different from them?
4. What do you do with your free time?
   a. What do you like about these activities, and what do you get from them?
5. What is your favourite motto or saying OR what saying would you have printed on a t-shirt?
   a. Why do you like that motto?
   b. What would be different if you lived your life more according to that saying?

As with so many career exercises, the value is not in the questions or the answers, but in the analysis and reflection you get your client to do afterwards. Most of these questions can reveal something about what really matters to them, and what kind of life they want to lead but you do need to spend time with them getting them to unpick what they think their answers say about them. Make sure you ask your client what they feel their answers say about their values, and use them as a starting point for a conversation about their identity and what a well-lived life would look like for them.

Key takeaways

Our lives are full of stories that we tell ourselves.

Career counselling can help clients to understand the stories they are telling, and to work out what story they want to be in and what character they want to play.

Careers are all about what matters and stories can help clients to identify their own values.

Career AdaptAbilities

Introduction

One of the important ideas contained within Career Construction Theory is career adaptability. Adaptability refers to the ability to identify and prepare for change, so career adaptability is about looking ahead and planning next steps in the context of a changing labour market landscape and changing lives. There are some obvious and predictable moments for career transition – most of us move from education to work, from one job to another and from work to retirement. But people may also encounter a range of less predictable career transitions, as they are made redundant, get promoted, or as a new boss, a new client or new technology forces a change. Other life transitions too can have a sometimes surprising impact on work, such as the birth of a child, a partner's new job or a bereavement or illness. We all need to work on our career adaptability to make sure that whatever life throws at us, we have the resources needed to anticipate the changes where we can, and respond positively.

The four Cs model

The four Cs model offers a framework to help, outlining four key characteristics that we need in order to be career adaptable. The four Cs are: *Curiosity, Concern, Confidence* and *Control*. Let us take each in turn.

Career curiosity is needed to generate good ideas. We need to be curious about our own futures, thinking about who we might be – our future work selves – and wondering what kinds of roles or positions or industries would satisfy us. As part of this we need to keep learning about different jobs, and finding out what options are out there, and to keep reflecting on ourselves, what matters to us, what our options are and where we could fit.

Career concern encourages us to plan. We need to be aware of the transitions that may be coming up and give ourselves time to prepare. This might include researching different options, talking to professionals who might be able to help, and arranging some work experience or job shadowing. It could

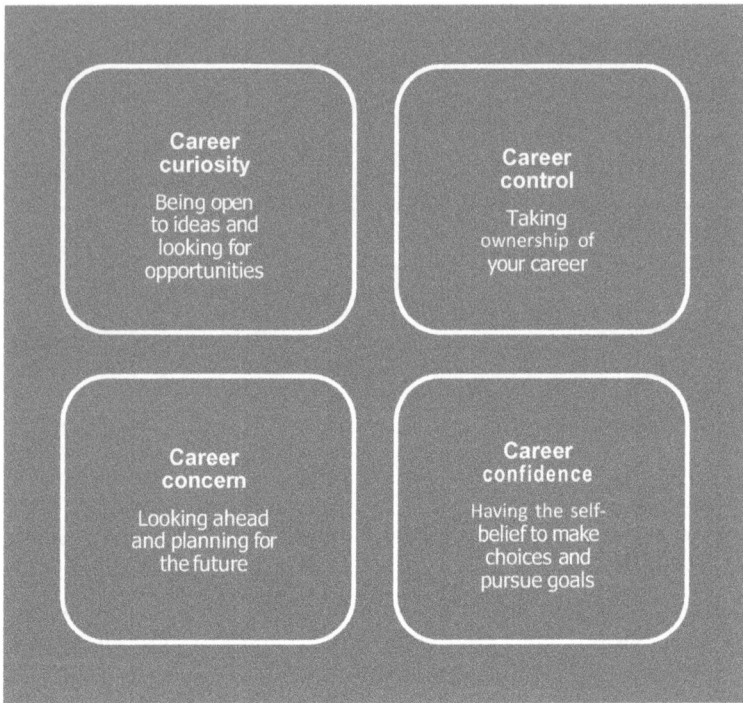

Figure 8.3 Savickas and Porfeli's model of Career AdaptAbilities.

also include an understanding of the chances of success and time identifying a Plan B, should things not move as quickly as we anticipate.

Career confidence allows us to aim high and helps us to achieve. I covered confidence (or self-efficacy) in the previous chapter, but the focus here is on its pivotal role in allowing us to identify goals that are meaningful to us, and giving us the resources and motivation to persist and work towards them despite any setbacks we might encounter.

Career control is a sense of agency. We can increase our career control by working out what we have power over and what we don't, and focusing on changing the things that we can and accepting those that we can't. A related concept you might have come across before is the idea of the *Locus of Control*. People have a natural tendency for a locus of control that is either internal or external. An *internal locus of control* means that you generally believe that events are in your own hands: if you are late, that is because you didn't leave enough time, if you do well on an exam, that is because you worked hard. An *external locus of control* means that your instinct is to lay the blame or credit externally – you were late because the traffic was bad, or you did well on the exam because the questions were easy. An internal locus of control is something to try and cultivate because it generally leads people to be more motivated, put more effort in to achieving their goals and to cope better in the face of setbacks.

Career AdaptAbilities in practice

To raise awareness
Share this model directly with your clients (either in group sessions or one-to-ones) and explain that these are the four key psychological resources that they need to develop in order to stand a good chance of being able to plan their careers, identify meaningful career goals and secure the jobs they want.

Practical exercises
Ask your clients to reflect on their current levels of each of the four Cs. There is a questionnaire that you can find online that you can use to help your clients work out where their strengths are and what might need further attention. Alternatively you could just describe the four Cs and ask your clients to rate themselves on each aspect.

You can use exercises as part of a career education group session, or suggest them to your client as part of a one-to-one conversation.

1) *Career concern*: Visualisation exercises that focus on clients' future identities can help them to work out what they want in their future and to stir them to action. The practice box below outlines a Possible Selves visualisation technique.

2) *Career curiosity*: You can use stories to pique clients' interest in finding out more about different opportunities. Identify a range of case studies which are going to feel relevant and relatable for your clients.

3) *Career confidence*: I give some suggestions for boosting confidence in the section on self-efficacy theory in Chapter 7, but one useful approach is to offer opportunities for clients to get some real-world practice – for example mock interviews, delivering a presentation or doing some work experience.

4) *Career control*: You can encourage your client to try and increase their internal locus of control. This involves helping them to become aware of their natural locus of control and then making a conscious effort to change or at least broaden some of their thinking. You might need to explain the concept to your client in the first instance and encourage them to consider where their locus of control usually lies. You could then invite them to think about a time where things didn't go so well for them, and invite them to think about what they could have done to improve their chances. When thinking about their future steps, encourage them to make a conscious effort to focus just on what they are in control of, rather than the factors outside their control.

Practice tip

Possible Selves is a visualisation technique that helps people to imagine themselves in the future and has been shown to help with goal setting and motivation. A possible self is an imagined version of yourself in the future. We all have multiple possible selves – different versions of ourselves we could be or different lives we could lead. One thing that makes this technique particularly effective is that it is focused on identity – who you could be, not what you could do.

Part 1: Visualise a possible self

Invite your client to think about themselves in the future – perhaps two or five years from now. Ask them to close their eyes and conjure up an image of this future self in their minds eye. When they have done this, ask them to describe this image, giving as much detail as they can. Ask open questions, encourage them to talk and then prompt them to fill in details where needed. Your job here is to help them imagine this future in as much vivid detail as you can.

Ask them a series of questions aimed at getting them to build up, explore and crystalise all aspects of this future. Here are some of the questions I often use, but do feel free to go with the flow here – you can base your conversation on what your client says, helping them to develop their own thoughts, or draw on other things you know about their values and interests.

> *Where are you working? What's the culture like in this workplace? How would you describe the environment?*
> *Who are you working with? What are your relationships like?*
> *When you arrive in the morning, what's the first thing you do? What's next?*
> *What do you wear to work?*
> *How do you feel about going into work in the mornings?*
> *When you tell people what you do, how do you feel?*
> *What are your weekends like these days?*
> *What do your family think about your new job?*
> *What is the thing that's most different from your current you?*

Part 2: Call to action

When you feel that you have gone down this route as far as it will go – when they have described this future life in as much detail as they can – ask them to open their eyes. At this point they are still half in the future and half in the present, and now is the time that they can capitalise on this close link to make an action plan. Ask them what is the first thing that they need to do in order to get started on their journey to this future possible self, and encourage them to think about this particular action quite specifically, covering exactly what they are going to do, when they might do it and how they could overcome any possible barriers.

This is an approach which can be used in groups as well as in one-to-one settings. In a group setting, I ask people to work in pairs, coaching each other, and I challenge the 'coach' to try and find as much detail as they can from their 'client' during the session. The group sessions of course carry some aspect of risk about them, and you need to spend a bit more time setting up the exercise at the start, and providing some opportunity for follow-up sessions, should they be needed afterwards, but it can definitely work well.

Key takeaways

The modern workplace is characterised by rapid change and workers need to be able to respond to and cope with change to ensure that they survive and thrive across their whole career.

There are four competencies that make up Career AdaptAbility (the four Cs): Concern, Curiosity, Confidence and Control.

If clients can boost their levels of all four, they are more likely to be able to make the most of their careers.

Chapter 9
Theories to explain the process of career decision-making

Overview

The process of career decision-making, as we know, is complex. The theories introduced in this chapter can help us make sense of the process and identify where clients typically get stuck. The theories can be useful in helping us to understand the process and perhaps share in a career conversation.

The three theories are:

- *Social Cognitive Career Theory,* which focuses on the interaction between individual and environmental factors.
- *System 1 and 2 Thinking,* which explains the difference between an unconscious intuitive approach and a conscious rational approach to decision-making.
- *Career Inaction Theory,* which identifies the particular contexts that can prevent people from moving forward.
- *Real-world Model of Career Decision-Making,* which shows how people actually decide on an occupation.

Introduction

In this chapter, we are going to look at four theories that explain the process of career decision-making. This is no mean feat. We know that career development is highly complex and also enormously variable – each of us has our own career development story, and the subtleties and details will vary considerably from one person to another, and from one life stage to another. Nevertheless, this is an extremely important category of theory. Research tells us that young people find the whole idea of thinking about career development stressful, and one reason for this is that they just don't know how to go about it or where to start. A recent study also showed that as career professionals, we aren't even always completely clear ourselves about how to explain this complicated and highly nuanced process to our clients. And a theory can really come into its own when we are trying to make sense of something very complicated.

We have four models to look at in this section: Social Cognitive Career Theory (SCCT) by Lent, Brown and Hackett; the System 1 and System 2 model of decision-making by Daniel Kahneman; Verbruggen and De Vos' Career Inaction Theory; and finally my own Real-world Model of Career Decision-Making. Each of these models looks at the process of career development from a different angle. The SCCT is a broad career theory that focuses on how different influences interact and lead to career choices. Kahneman's model of decision-making – System 1 and System 2 – highlights the two key cognitive approaches to decision-making. Career Inaction Theory shows us why and where people can get stuck with their career planning, and finally the Real-World Model offers a four-stage model showing how people actually make their career decisions.

Social Cognitive Career Theory

Introduction

This model was developed in 1994, in the US, by vocational psychologists Lent, Brown and Hackett. It is probably (definitely) the model that is most widely used in academic career research, clocking up more than 10,000 academic citations. But despite its dominance in the academic literature, it is surprisingly unfamiliar to many of us and is rarely applied in career practice.

Its popularity in the academic world is probably because it is comprehensive and very well evidenced. But the lack of engagement with it in the world of practice could also be a result of the same two factors: it's so comprehensive that it can feel a bit overwhelming, and it's well evidenced because it uses some quite specific psychological ideas which are well trodden in the academic world, but which don't necessarily mean much to those of us working in practice.

Nevertheless, I think it deserves some attention, so I will now have a go at describing it.

The first two boxes on the left of the diagram above are all about influences, and they highlight that career development is influenced by both personal factors and family background. Personal factors are many and varied. They include personality, values, interests, strengths, intelligence, sexuality, gender, age and appearance. Family background covers all sorts of things linked to where you were born and who you were born to. It includes social

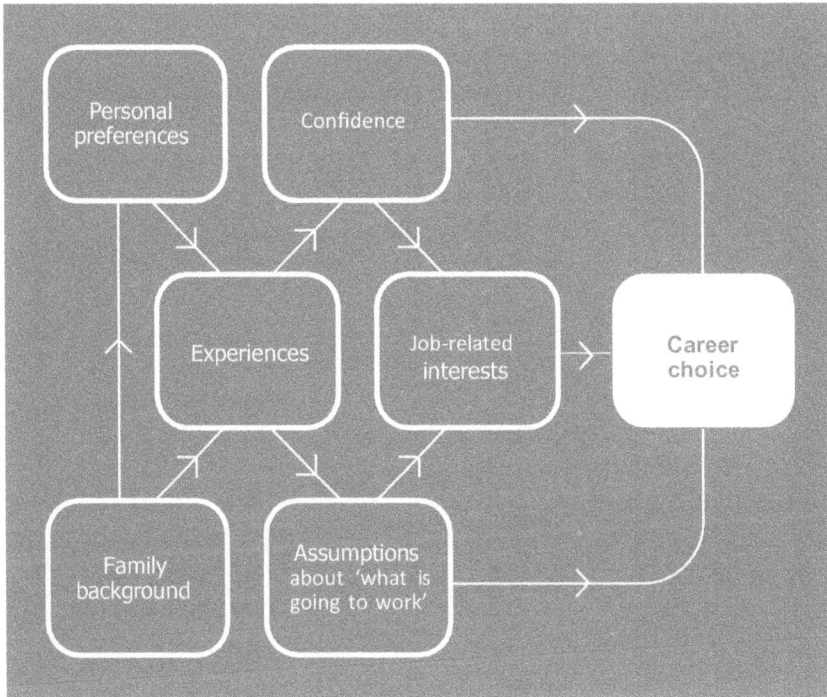

Figure 9.1 Lent et al.'s Social Cognitive Career Theory.

class, geographical location, parental values and siblings. You will see in the diagram that there is an arrow pointing from family background to personal factors. This acknowledges the way that we are shaped by our environment – almost every aspect of who we are is shaped, to some degree, by where we are from. Take values, for example. Our values – what matters to us in life and within our careers – are our own, but they are influenced by our parents and informed by the experiences we have as children. Of course, we don't always embrace our parents' values wholesale – in fact, sometimes we move quite consciously in a different direction – but the first set of values we espouse tends to be highly informed by our parents' values, which in turn will be influenced by their culture and community.

Next, we move on to 'experiences', and you can see in the diagram that they are influenced by both our personal factors and family background. Who we are and where we are from have an impact on our experiences. Of course, they do. Our parents choose where we live, who gets invited to our home and where we go to school, and our society has an impact on the toys we play with, the television shows that we watch and the activities we do. But our own preferences also have an impact, and as we get older, we start to determine more of these choices for ourselves, making our own decisions about who we spend time with, which subjects we study and how we spend our leisure time.

When it comes to work-specific experiences, the first careers we are exposed to are those of the people around us; we find out what our parents do, and we learn about doctors, teachers, shop workers and bus drivers from our own experiences. We might also have our own early taste of work – perhaps through a part-time job, volunteering or school work experiences. The nature of these experiences is often determined by a combination of individual and environmental factors – we might hear about a part-time job through a friend or through our parents, but we might also be able to make some of our own choices, opting for work experience in construction rather than in an office because we enjoy practical work or choosing a part-time job in a clothes shop rather than a supermarket because of an interest in fashion.

These experiences then inform our career choices through two mechanisms. The first is that they have an impact on our confidence. Any kind of success or compliment can make us feel more capable. Positive feedback from a customer during work experience might make us feel that we are good at working with people; a good mark on a maths test might make us feel that we have some natural aptitude with numbers; a compliment about a drawing we have done might boost our sense of our own creativity.

The second mechanism through which our experience influences our choices is that it informs our assumptions about the impact of different behaviours: the kinds of actions that lead to particular outcomes (described as 'outcome expectations' in the academic literature). A child in an aspirational school might learn that working hard at school will get them to university, which will lead to a good job. A child whose parents are happy in their jobs will learn that work is something that will lead to fulfilment. An adolescent whose hard work during their work experience leads to an offer for a part-time job will learn that putting in the effort can result in opportunities.

The next link is a really important one. The combination of confidence and outcome expectations leads to career interests. People take an interest in jobs when a) they feel they might have the skills or aptitude to do them, and b) where they can imagine doing what is needed to attain them. This is really important because it shows that just having an interest in a field does not determine a job interest. The bit about confidence is perhaps more obvious – of course people aren't going to pursue career fields that they don't think they could manage. But it's important to remember that confidence isn't always the same as aptitude. Our clients can sometimes be under-confident and make a choice not to go for an opportunity they are actually well equipped for.

Here are some examples of how confidence and outcome expectations can inform career interests:

- I love football, but I'm not very talented (confidence). I am also not prepared to put in the kind of effort needed, and I know my chances would be very slim anyway (outcome expectations), so I'm not going to consider pursuing it.

- I am really good at French at school (confidence), but I don't see how a degree would benefit me (outcome expectations), so I am not considering further study.

- I did really well during my work experience at the local school (confidence), and I know that I stand a good chance of being able to become a primary teacher by going to university (outcome expectations), so I'm planning to do that.

- I know I've got a good range of skills (confidence), but my chances of getting on a graduate training scheme with an investment bank are really slim (outcome expectations), so I'm not going to apply.

- My science marks are actually really good, but I just don't feel that I've got what it takes to get onto a degree course in medicine (confidence).

The last part of the model takes the three ideas of job-related interests, confidence and outcome expectations (assumptions about what is going to work) and shows how they lead to career choices. In essence, this last stage highlights that people choose to go for jobs that they think they will find interesting, that they believe they will be good at, and where they can see what they need to do to be successful.

SCCT in practice

To deepen your understanding of influences:

Simply having a clear sense of the key elements of the model can help you as a practitioner reach a deeper understanding of your clients. Remembering that their job interests will be determined and constrained by a combination of their individual characteristics, environmental backgrounds and experiences can help you see how they have ended up where they are now.

To identify a direction for practice:

The model can help you keep the two ideas of confidence and outcome expectations clear in your mind.

Confidence is so important in so many different ways – do make sure that you capitalise on any opportunity to boost your client's confidence by encouraging them to identify their own strengths, skills, achievements and resources. There are some lovely techniques from positive psychology that can help you, and do go back to Chapter 7 for ideas for boosting clients' confidence.

The idea of outcome expectations (a client's sense of the outcomes that certain actions lead to) is also a useful one to remember in practice. We know that our clients often have a limited understanding of the labour market, the world of work or the application process. Clients will also often have a biased or flawed understanding of these factors – we pick up most of our career information from informal sources which are often highly subjective or personal (and sometimes wrong). The idea of outcome expectations reminds us to talk to our clients about what they know, what their views are and also to help them unpick where those assumptions have come from to determine how valid they might be.

To share with clients explicitly:

It's a complicated model, and I wouldn't necessarily suggest you start describing the whole thing from start to finish within a one-to-one conversation. However, it could be a useful model to share with some clients as part of a more in-depth career education programme. The model in its entirety could illustrate the complexity of the whole process of career development, or perhaps you could use certain elements of it to make a particular point. For example, just focus on the first three boxes (personal factors, family background and experiences) as the starting point for an exercise to encourage your clients to identify how their own preferences have been influenced by their families and how their career learning has been shaped by a combination of their environment and their personality. Alternatively, you could focus on the confidence aspect more explicitly, using its central role here as a starting point for a session on confidence, encouraging your clients to think about where their career confidence comes from and introducing some specific techniques to boost it.

Key takeaways

Careers are determined by a combination of individual factors (such as abilities, personality and values) and environmental factors (including family, social class and location);

This combination of personal and environmental factors influences our experiences.

Confidence is at the heart of career decision-making – we like doing things we are good at.

An important issue is the assumptions we develop about what kinds of actions will lead to which kinds of outcomes.

System 1 and System 2

Introduction

This one isn't a career-specific theory, but it is an approach that I find really helpful and is one that can easily be applied to a career context. Kahneman was a psychologist who spent his life trying to understand how we make decisions. He concluded that we have two separate cognitive systems that we use to make decisions: one (System 1) that you might describe as your gut instinct and the other (System 2) that is a more conscious rational approach. The two systems often function entirely independently but work best when they are combined. And this is something that we can help our clients with.

System 1

System 1 is our gut instinct, which has evolved over thousands of years to enable us to take in and process enormous amounts of information in an instant and to make reasonably good judgements and decisions with minimal effort. System 1 has some particular strengths. It can cope with enormous amounts of information and process it all quickly. It is able to make sense of imperfect or incomplete information. And it is also really good at thinking about creative solutions when there is no obvious 'right' answer.

You can see why this is so useful for career choices. The amount of information we have about careers is immense. The government in the UK recognises an eye-watering 29,000 different job titles – it clearly takes an inordinate amount of cognitive processing to reduce that down to one. And then the information we have about these occupations is also varied, incomplete and generally a bit unreliable. And there is no right answer. System 1 is very much the best approach for navigating through this kind of chaos.

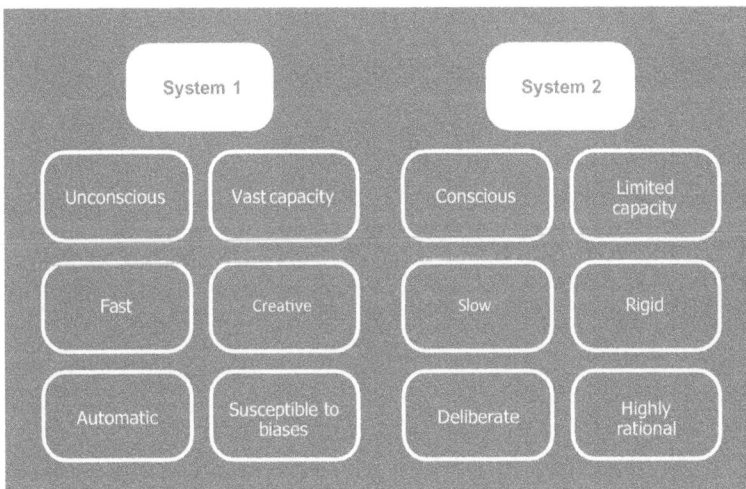

Figure 9.2 Kahneman's System 1 and System 2 thinking.

System 2

This is a newer addition to our cognitive toolkit, having evolved much more recently, and is a slower, more consciously rational approach. You could argue that this system is not as good. It can't process as much information, it takes far longer and it requires a lot of mental effort to work. But it is much more logical and less likely to be influenced by flattery, charisma or familiarity.

System 2 is conscious, and the bit of the brain that deals with conscious processes is far smaller than the part that processes intuition. As such, System 2 can only cope with small amounts of information. It also requires deliberate thought and effort: you need to choose to think about a particular scenario with your System 2 brain, whereas your System 1 thinking happens automatically. But while System 2 is slow, demanding and limited, it is also more rational. It doesn't draw on stereotypes or on flawed information; it doesn't assume that the charismatic speaker is telling the truth, and it doesn't make up information where it can't find it. Arguably, System 2 makes better decisions, but it only works well when the choices are limited and complete, comprehensive accurate information is available.

Dual-Processing

Both approaches have their strengths and limitations, but if we understand how they work and make an effort to combine the two approaches, we can capitalise on the benefits of both.

System 1 can't be switched off. It's always whirring away in the background, and you can't not have an instinctive opinion. What is important is that you recognise that, and try to identify what your instinct is telling you. If you can bring your System 1 rationale forward into the conscious part of your brain, then you can start to think about it rationally. In this way, you can capitalise on System 1's ability to take in and process lots of information quickly, but at the same time take advantage of System 2's logic. Once you are consciously aware of your instinctive opinion, you can use your System 2 to scrutinise it.

System 1 and System 2 in practice

This understanding of decision-making styles can be used with clients facing two quite different kinds of decision-making issues.

With clients who are struggling to make a decision

We sometimes work with clients who are facing a decision and don't know which way to turn. Distinguishing between their System 1 and System 2 thought processes can shed some light on their motives and help unlock them.

- Using the language of 'head and heart', ask your client to tell you what their heart (System 1) is saying and what their head (System 2) is saying.
- Ask your clients about a previous good decision they made. Ask them whether they made it logically and rationally (System 2) or by going with their gut instinct (System 1). Then suggest that they think about their current dilemma solely with that approach.

With clients whose choices concern you

Our clients, of course, should and will make their own choices. We wholeheartedly buy into the idea that our clients know themselves better than we do and have every right to make their own choices. But as practitioners, we sometimes think that our clients might not be making decisions based on the strongest rationale. You might, for example, see a client who seems to be making a choice because they have been swayed by a charismatic or flattering inspirational figure. That is not to say that this is necessarily the wrong choice for your client, but if you know about the dark arts of System 1 thinking and you believe it might be working its magic in an unhelpful way, then it is completely appropriate that you, gently, tentatively and sensitively raise this with your client.

In these cases, you might want to explain the two systems to your client in simple terms. You can then ask them to tell you which of the two systems is most strongly advocating for this particular choice. Invite them to try and articulate the rationale for the choice – what is System 1 telling them, and why is it talking in these terms? You can then invite them to take the perspective of the other system and ask them to explore the alternative perspective. This might lead to a client feeling even more confident about their earlier choice or might make them realise that they need to do a bit more research or thinking before they are ready to make up their minds.

I find it helpful to talk about System 1 and System 2 as external beings: I might say something like, '*What is your System 1 telling you?*' rather than '*What are you thinking?*'. This way, I can set up a narrative in which the client and I together are scrutinising their System 1 thinking. It can be easier for us both to critique it if we are imagining it as somewhat distinct from the client themselves.

Key takeaways

We have two cognitive decision-making systems: System 1 – our gut instinct, and System 2 – our conscious rational logic.

System 1 is great because it can cope with large amounts of information and can be creative, but it is susceptible to biases.

System 2 is less susceptible to biases. and a bit more reliable.

But it gets a bit overwhelming when there is too much information or when the information isn't all complete.

Combining the two approaches usually leads to the best decisions.

Career Inaction Theory

Introduction
We have all seen clients who are unmotivated: clients who might know where they want to get to, and might even know exactly what they need to do to get there, but just can't seem to motivate themselves to put their plans into action. Career Inaction Theory offers us some insights which might explain what is going on.

This is a career-specific theory, but the authors were inspired by the literature in a sub-discipline of psychology which focuses on 'doing nothing'. The doing-nothing psychologists have identified a particular set of circumstances described as inertia-enhancing mechanisms – particular contexts that are likely to stop people from moving forward. Verbruggen and De Vos, our career inaction theorists, realised that these particular circumstances are very common within career development and developed their Career Inaction Theory to help explain why some clients get stuck.

Inertia-enhancing mechanisms
There are three key inertia-enhancing mechanisms. Each of these can lead to inaction, and as you will recognise, each of them is very common in career development.

Fear and anxiety
The first of the three inertia-enhancing mechanisms is fear and anxiety. We know that these negative emotions are very common during career decisions. We see a lot of career anxiety in our clients, and we know that people find a number of different aspects of career planning unsettling. People find the whole process daunting; they fear not being able to make a decision, or making the wrong decision; they are worried that they are falling behind

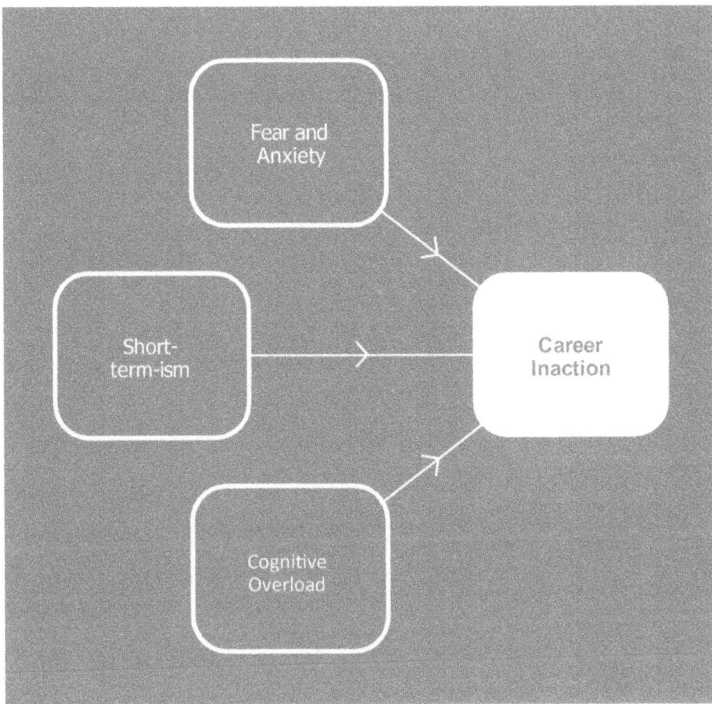

Figure 9.3 Verbruggen and De Vos' Career Inaction Theory.

their peers; they worry that they might not do the job well or that they will be miserable in it. They know that whatever choice they make will carry a risk, and sometimes it just feels safer to stop thinking about it.

Short term-ism

A career move almost always entails some kind of short-term sacrifice. A new job might have the potential to be more satisfying and stimulating, but it might well come at the expense of a safe environment – a familiar office, a regular routine or a kind colleague. A student might know that they need to find a job once their course finishes, but writing an application form, preparing a presentation and attending an interview are very time-consuming, and focusing on them might entail a sacrifice of leisure time. Sometimes, this just doesn't feel worth it, and it can be very tempting to postpone your career planning to a later date.

Cognitive overload

Our minds are wonderful places, but as we identified in the last section, our conscious rational brains can easily get overloaded. Career choices are highly complex, involving many different career or job options, dozens of factors to consider and endless relevant (and sometimes not so relevant) information to research and understand. Sophisticated as they are, our brains can find this all utterly overwhelming, and this cognitive overload can lead us to shut down and stop engaging.

Career Inaction Theory in practice
Fear and anxiety

One reason for clients' lack of confidence in their own ability to make a good choice is because they don't have any good role models whose stories can make them feel optimistic about their own futures. Ask your client to try and think about people they know who have been in a similar situation and have managed to move forward. They might think about older siblings, course alumni or co-workers. Encourage them to tell these stories, reflect on any challenges these people faced and talk about how they overcame them. Even if those people have not ended up in perfect jobs, perhaps your client might be able to see that they have at least moved on and might be able to spot some positive outcomes. Sometimes a client might not be able to identify a relatable role model. In these situations, it is useful to have a few case studies of your own to draw on. Think about some other clients you yourself have worked with and use their (anonymised) stories to give your clients some hope.

Short term-ism

One useful approach to dealing with short term-ism is to try and ensure that your client has a crystal-clear vision of their own future. Spending some time getting them to visualise their own future can be a useful way to make the future seem both more promising and a bit closer. One good visualisation technique is 'possible selves', where you ask your client to imagine themselves 5 or 10 years in the future and ask them to describe their lives (see Chapter 8, page 76 for a detailed description). Your goal as the career professional here is to get them to paint a vivid picture of their future, encouraging your client to really start to feel what it would be like to be that future version of themselves.

Cognitive overload

One approach for dealing with cognitive overload is to try and encourage your client to rely more on their System 1 thinking. In the previous section, I described the limited processing capacity of System 2 (your conscious rational brain), in contrast to the almost limitless power of System 1 (your unconscious gut instinct). Cognitive overload will always be a risk with the System 2 brain, so encouraging your client to switch over to their System 1 brain can be the key to unsticking the stuckness. Help your client to work out what their gut instinct has to say, and use that as a starting point for a discussion about the right next steps.

Another approach to managing cognitive overload is to try and get your client to break everything down into bite-sized, manageable tasks. I sometimes use sticky notes to help with this. I ask my client to write down every single thing they need to consider or do – one task per sticky note. My client then puts the sticky notes on the table in front of them. Even this first simple step can be a relief as the client has taken the messy, panicking ideas swirling around in their heads and organised them into a set of single, manageable tasks. Then, ask them to put the sticky notes in order – placing them in a line from left to right in the order in which they need to be addressed – the first task on the left through to the last task on the right. Then, get them to pile the sticky notes up, in order, with the last task on the bottom through to the first task on the top. Your client then has a single pile of tasks that contains everything they have to do, but on top they can just see one single task. This is then their to-do list – they need to work through one at a time, just doing the single task on the top and removing the sticky note once it is done.

Key takeaways

Career decisions often involve some anxiety, short-term sacrifices and too much information.

These factors can lead to career inaction.

Role models can help people feel more confident.

A visualisation exercise can help people focus more on the future.

Breaking the tasks down into a step-by-step approach can help with cognitive overload.

Real-World Model of Career Decision-Making

The theories we cover in this book look at all sorts of different and important aspects of career development, and the career literature over the years has given us lots of insights into what influences us, what helps us and hinders us, how our career paths develop and how we learn about careers. But none of the theories seem to give us a clear model to explain how people actually make decisions – a step-by-step guide to explain how people go from '*I have no idea*' to '*I'm now working*'.

Frustrated by this, I set about doing some research with graduates to find out how they actually made their choices, and on the back of that research, I developed this model. It has a lot in common with some of the more traditional approaches, but there are some clear differences, which seem to resonate with clients. It also offers a step-by-step process which can be helpful to share with young people who are just starting to think about their

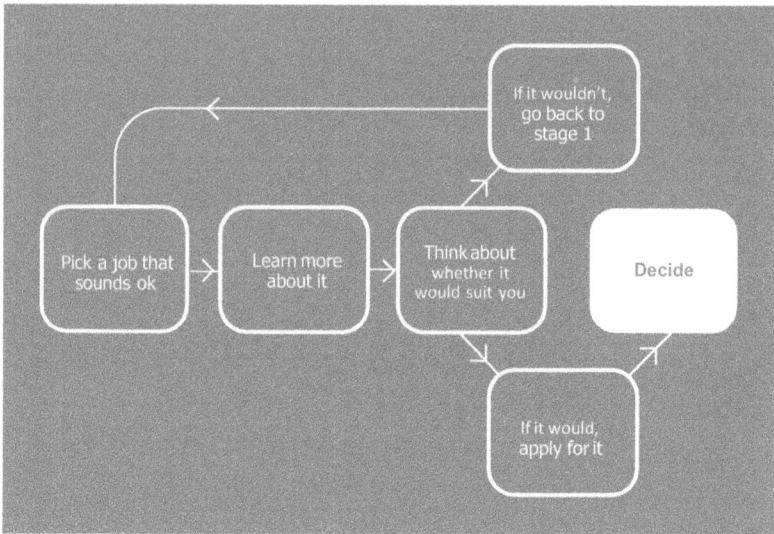

Figure 9.4 The Real-World Model of Career Decision-Making.

own choices. While the model was developed through conversations with graduates, I think it resonates with other clients making their first career choices.

Five stages of Career Decision-Making

The model involves five stages. These can be iterative – that is, clients might go back and forth between stages or find themselves going around in circles a bit, going through some of the first four stages more than once before they make a decision. Clients can also be at different stages of the model with different job ideas at the same time.

Stage 1: Pick a job that sounds okay. The starting point is to identify one job that sounds reasonably interesting. This job can come from anywhere – perhaps it's an idea from social media or a school subject, perhaps the individual was inspired by some work experience they did or a conversation with a friend or family member. It might even have come from a careers event or a discussion with a career professional.

Stage 2: Learn more about it. Next, they do some research. This could include some internet research, a conversation with someone they might know who actually does the job or some work experience.

Stage 3: Think about whether the job is suitable. This is the point at which people really start thinking about themselves and whether this particular job would meet their needs and suit their character. If they decide it's not right for them, they go back to Stage 1 and look for another job to think about. If they think it might be suitable, they move on to Stage 4.

Stage 4: Apply. The application process for many people is part of their exploration. Some may have decided for sure before they apply, but for many, the application process is a way to learn more, giving them an opportunity to meet people who work in the field and a chance to get a feel for the organisation and its culture.

Stage 5: Decide. For many, it is only then, once they have actually applied for the job, that they make a decision. And even then, many of them aren't sure. Often, people start working in a job that will keep their options open and stay just until they know whether to stick with it or look for something different. For many young people choosing their first occupation, it's a case of *apply and then decide*; not *decide and then apply*.

What's new?

The stages in this model are, to some degree, familiar. The process of having an idea, exploring it in depth and making a choice is well-worn. But there are some key differences between the stages in this model and more traditional advice.

1). *Young people think about career ideas one at a time.* They don't (as traditional models advise) come up with a shortlist and then explore them all to identify the best one. Instead, they pick one job idea, explore it and decide whether it's a yes or a no. If it's a no, they go back and pick another.

Career choices are incredibly complex, and one thing that causes decision-making paralysis is cognitive overload – when you have too much to think about at once (see Career Inaction Theory earlier in the chapter for more on this). Taking one job idea at a time seems to keep the process manageable.

2). *Self-awareness happens in the context of a particular job idea.* Young people don't start by thinking about themselves, their strengths, values and requirements. Instead, they start with a job idea and then reflect on themselves in terms of that one idea. They might, for example, pick the idea of nursing and then ask themselves, 'What would I like about nursing? What would I not like? What would I be good at? What would I struggle with?' They seem to find it easier to answer *'What would you like or dislike about being a nurse?'* than *'What would you like or dislike in a job?'*.

Again, this seems very practical. We all know that becoming self-aware is a lifetime endeavour, and for these young people with their limited life and work experience, answering abstract questions about their strengths and values is nearly impossible. Placing these same questions within a tangible context – one that they can imagine or envisage – makes it far easier.

3) *Students explore occupational ideas by applying for a job.* Traditional models suggest that decision-makers should explore, make a choice and then apply; but in reality, people often explore their job ideas through applying, and then make a choice.

This makes some sense, although it has its down sides. The interview process is a great way to talk to people working in the field and can really help young people imagine themselves in that position. But the danger is that they use the application process as a way to avoid having to make a choice – they leave the 'choice' in the hands of the employer, seeing a job offer as a sign that the job is right for them, or perhaps feeling that they have invested so much in the application process that they couldn't bear their efforts to be wasted. The idea of applying as a way to find out more feels like an approach that could be useful, as long as the young people resist the temptation just to accept their first offer.

4)) *Keep your options open.* Young people starting out in the labour market may have settled on an occupation and have started working, but for many of them, it won't feel like a conclusion. It's just something to do while they carry on looking.

This feels like a very reassuring message to give young people. Career anxiety is widespread among young people, and one of their main fears is that they will make the wrong choice. This model shows that there is no wrong choice. Even if they end up doing something terrible, somewhere they hate, it doesn't matter. They will learn something, earn some money and be in a position to make a better choice next time around.

The Real-World Model in practice

1. *To illustrate how career decisions are made.* Sharing this model explicitly in a one-to-one career conversation or at the start of a career education programme can show clients how it's done, reassure them that the process is completely manageable and give them a place to start.

2. *As a structure for careers education – helping you to get your input in the right order.* This model shows us that it's far easier for our clients to think

about themselves in the context of a particular job. Asking '*What do you want in a job?*' is a far harder question to answer than '*What would you like or dislike about being a police officer?*'. So starting your career education sessions with a look at options is better than starting with self-awareness. Your clients don't at all need to commit to a particular option at the start, but they will have an instinctive view about which jobs sound vaguely interesting and which don't.

- ✔ First, identify five occupations to focus on. You could pick the five most common destinations of people from your clients' school or university course.

- ✔ Give your clients an overview of each of them – perhaps presenting a case study of one particular person to make it relatable. Then, ask your clients to pick one or two that they are drawn to and give them a job description for each to look at.

- ✔ Ask them to identify the aspects of the job that they imagine they would like, and those that they wouldn't. Get them to think about which parts of the job they would be good at, and which parts they wouldn't. Help them to work out which of those aspects of the job they feel strongly about.

- ✔ Get them to think about next steps. Does the job seem like a good match? Should they try to find out more? What do they want to know and how could they find that information? If the job doesn't sound like a good fit, what does that tell them about themselves and what they want, or don't want, in a job? And is there another job they might want to move on to thinking about next?

3. *To help clients improve their career decision-making.* This is a descriptive theory, not a prescriptive one – this means that it explains how people actually make their choices, as opposed to offering a model for making *good* choices. It can be useful for you to be aware of the flaws in this approach so that you can look out for opportunities to improve some of your clients' thinking. For example, you might want to look for opportunities to encourage your clients to broaden their horizons, help people to find better ways to gather information beyond just talking to friends and add an objective, scrutinising layer to their decision-making to make sure they aren't only swayed by their System 1 thinking.

THE REAL-WORLD MODEL WITH GRADUATES

Anjli Shah

A lot of the one-to-one work that I do is with graduates, and I use this model quite often. I find that it really helps with self-awareness, and it's useful both for exploring career ideas to find the right one and to help them with their job hunting.

So, for instance, a typical graduate might come and say, '*I've made hundreds of applications and I've had no success. I have not even been getting through to the second stage; I'm just getting rejections.*' And the first thing I do is explore what they've been applying for and what their ideas are. They do generally start with some focused career thoughts, but because they haven't really thought about themselves in relation to that particular job, their applications are not as tailored as they could be.

We pick one of their career ideas to explore and look for a live application and find the job description and person specification. Then, we spend time actually decoding that job, working out what they would actually do if they were doing the job and thinking about whether it would suit them. The model stresses that it's easier to think about self-awareness in the context of a specific job – easier to think about '*What would I like about being an investment banker?*' than '*What do I want from a job?*'. In decoding that job, we make it really real, really tangible. We focus on questions like '*What would it feel like to work in this? What have you done so far that will demonstrate the transferability into this job, the skill set?*' and thinking about their career ideas in this way – using a specific live job application – just seems to make it real for them. They can really imagine what it would be like to do that job, and that helps them to make good decisions.

In every other career model that we use, self-awareness tends to come first – the other models (like the DOTS model, for instance) say that we should start the process of career exploration with self-awareness. But actually, I find that self-awareness only really starts to develop and deepen when you are looking at a specific opportunity – when your client can look at self-awareness in relation to a specific job. It makes it easier for them to understand themselves. Trying to understand themselves in a vacuum can be very difficult.

Using the job opportunity and the job description itself as a tangible context for developing self-awareness is useful both in terms of exploration – confirming whether this particular role is actually going to suit them – and in terms of actually getting jobs as well. That deeper self-awareness that is specific to the job really helps them to articulate their motivation clearly, explain why they're excited about the job and helps them to demonstrate that they understand the job well.

Key takeaways

Students and graduates tend to follow these five steps when they make their career choices:

1. They first pick a job that sounds vaguely interesting, and then they research it.

2. They consider whether it might suit them.

3. If it doesn't, they go back and pick another job.

4. If it sounds okay, they apply.

5. If they like what they learn during the application process and get offered a job, then they decide whether to take it.

A key thing to note is that students find it easier to think about self-awareness in the context of a particular job: it's easier to answer '*What bits of the job of a primary teacher would you do well?*' than '*What would you be good at in the workplace?*'

You can share this model with young people to illustrate the steps they need to take.

Chapter 10
Theories to enhance self-awareness

Overview

Self-awareness is fundamental to good career choices, and the deeper the self-awareness, the better. But we know that developing a sophisticated work-related self-awareness is not easy for our clients, particularly for young people who may have had limited exposure to the workplace.

In this chapter, I will introduce three theories that can help clients explore different aspects of their work selves:

- *Career Success*: which can help clients work out what they want from a career.
- *The RIASEC Hexagon*: a well-known matching approach to explore career interests.
- *Self-Determination Theory:* which can help clients to consider their own motivation.

Introduction

Self-awareness is, of course, fundamental to good career choices. Our clients will never be able to make informed, appropriate choices if they don't know who they are, what they want and what they are good at. At one level, our clients are often pretty good at this – most can think of some things that they are good at, or some kind of work that sounds appealing, or can tick things that matter to them on a list. But we know that they can sometimes struggle to delve deeper, to develop a more sophisticated work-relevant awareness of themselves in a work setting. This is more true with some clients than others, but we are seeing a decrease in the amount of time young people spend in the workplace, which really isn't helping. Many schools these days find that they can't offer work experience for their pupils, and on top of that, the proportion of young people with part-time jobs or volunteer positions has decreased significantly since the start of the century. The consequences for career decision-making are obvious – without time spent in the workplace, how can you begin to learn what it means to be a team player or what good workplace communication looks like? And how can you start to build up a sense of what is going to suit you in a job if you have no idea what work really feels like?

One obvious bit of advice to clients and anyone starting to think about their career choice is to get out there and try some things out. But, back to the focus of this chapter, we can also draw on some theories and models to help our clients structure their reflections.

There are many theories and models of self-awareness to choose from, and really, I would encourage you to use whichever ones seem to resonate with you and your clients. But here are three that might be worth exploring. I will start with the idea of career success. This is a model rather than a formal theory, but I find it extremely useful for exploring individual work-related values. Then I'm going to move on to Holland's classic matching theory, known as RIASEC, which looks at career interests. Finally, I will talk about Career Self-Determination Theory, which is a career-specific adaptation of a classic psychological theory that looks at motivation and the idea of psychological needs.

Career success

Introduction
There are three parts to this model: objective success, subjective success and job satisfaction. There are links between them, some of which are perhaps a little bit counter-intuitive. I will go on to talk about them later in the chapter, but first I want to take each of these three parts and explore them in a bit more depth.

Objective career success
Objective career success is the kind of success most of us imagine when we think about people who are 'successful' at work. It's the kind of success that is visible from the outside, and there are usually some shared social norms which shape our understanding of it – most people within a particular culture would probably have similar views on who has been 'successful' within their careers and who hasn't. It is most often defined in terms of pay and influence, so people who have large salaries, who have risen up the career ladder to senior positions and who seem to have a large reach – a large sphere of influence – are generally considered objectively successful in their careers.

There are a few key factors that lead to this kind of objective career success. People are more likely to become successful in this way if they are clever, if they work hard, if they are well networked (whether that is being born into

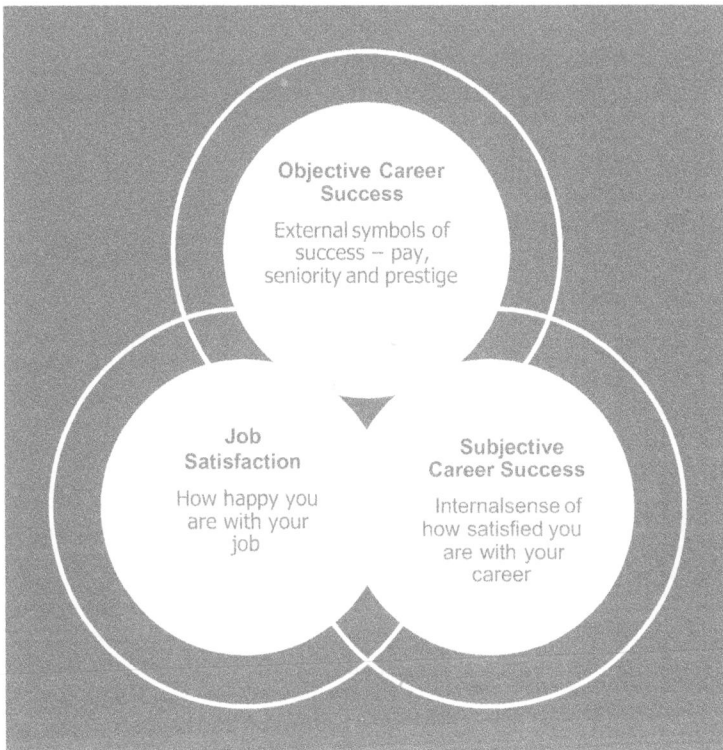

Figure 10.1 Model of career success.

the right networks or developing their own) and if they have what is known as a 'proactive personality' – which means someone who is dynamic and gets things done.

This is the aspect of career success that is most obvious, and I think there are often assumptions both within our society and within our clients that this is what we all want. I mean, who doesn't like the idea of being wealthy and important? But as we go through the other two aspects, I hope it becomes clear that notions of success aren't quite that straightforward.

Subjective career success

Subjective career success is a measure of how well you think you have done in your career. Your sense of subjective career success is generally a product of two different kinds of comparisons. First, you compare yourself to people around you. If you have a sense that you have done reasonably well compared to the people you know, then you will feel that you are a success. If you believe that other people around you are all doing better than you – earning more money and being promoted more quickly – then you will feel that you are not doing so well.

The second comparison is with your own expectations for yourself – a comparison between what you have achieved and what you thought you would achieve. If you have achieved what you imagined you would achieve, then you will feel you've done reasonably well. If you fall short of your own expectations, then you will feel you haven't been very successful.

Job satisfaction

Job satisfaction, then, is a different thing altogether. It's a fairly self-explanatory concept – usually measured in the academic world by a single question asking people, 'How satisfied do you feel with your job?' The research in this field suggests that there are two types of work satisfaction – both of which are important: feeling pleasure and feeling purpose.

Feeling pleasure is described as *hedonism* in the literature. This is just pure enjoyment and happiness, and it can come from a range of work-related things, including having a good chat or some banter with a colleague, having access to a nice canteen that serves delicious sandwiches, or going for work drinks.

Feeling purpose, known as *eudaimonia* in the literature, is linked to the sense that the job you are doing is connected to something bigger, something beyond you, and that your work is making a positive contribution. A good start to finding purpose in your work is to find something that aligns with your values, uses your strengths and allows you to be your own authentic self at work.

Both of these types of happiness are important, but eudaimonic pleasure tends to have a greater positive and lasting impact.

You can see then that career success overall is more complex and more individual than a simple measure of money and status. It also incorporates a measure of how well you personally feel that you are doing and a combination of how much fun you have at work and how meaningful your job is. These are much more personal and will be grounded in each individual's own values.

The links between the three elements

Subjective career success tends to lead to objective career success: people who feel that they are successful at work generally end up being promoted and getting pay raises. The explanation for this is that if you feel successful, you will be confident, and this confidence will encourage some of the behaviours that lead to objective career success, including proactivity, good networks and hard work.

Subjective career success also seems to lead to job satisfaction – this time through the link with eudaimonia. People who feel successful are likely to feel that they are making a difference, and this boosts their sense of purpose.

Job satisfaction then leads to objective career success – as with subjective career success, if you are feeling positive, you are more likely to work harder, be proactive and develop those useful networks – all of which make your objective success more likely.

There is a link between objective and subjective career success – people who are objectively successful do generally feel subjectively successful – they do realise that they have done well. But the link isn't very strong: rich, influential, senior people only feel a little bit more successful than the rest of us. This might seem a bit surprising, but there is a good explanation. You remember that subjective career success is all about comparisons? As your career progresses and you become more senior and better paid, your reference group changes. You stop comparing yourself to the people you've left behind and start comparing yourself to a new set of peers – who, inevitably, are just as well paid and just as influential as you are. Your yardstick to measure how well you've done changes, and you tend to judge yourself more harshly as you progress upwards.

Objective career success also has an impact on job satisfaction, but again, the relationship is a bit more complicated. Objective career success boosts job satisfaction through increased autonomy – senior people are more likely to make their own choices over what they do and how they do it, and we know that in general people like having some control over their own lives. But on the downside, the personal relationships senior managers have with their colleagues are generally not as fulfilling. We know that camaraderie – having a good bunch of colleagues you enjoy working with, and see and chat to on a daily basis – has an impact on workplace happiness, and as you get more senior, you tend to be a bit more isolated.

The message is that finding a job that you think matters and aligns with your values is likely to lead to a fulfilling and well-paid career, whereas a focus on objective career success at the expense of personal meaning may well make you less happy.

The career success model in practice
The notion of objective career success is so strong within our culture – it's such an ingrained assumption that we all aspire to wealth and influence that we almost don't realise that there are other ways to think about it. The key lesson from this model is that a successful career looks different for every one of us.

Share the model explicitly. In the first instance, you could share the model and get your clients to think about the difference between being 'successful' at work and being 'happy' at work.

Make it tangible. Ask your clients to try and identify two people they know, one of whom they would say is successful, and one of whom they think is happy at work. Ask them to think about these two people and talk about how they have defined 'success', and what similarities or differences they can see between the two.

Make it personal. You could then get them to start thinking about what is going to make them feel successful at work. If your clients have already had some experience in the world of work, you could get them to think about the job they've had that made them happiest. Invite them to analyse what made the job so good, and whether there was anything missing. You could also get them to think about their worst ever job and again analyse what they disliked about it.

Visualisation to identify values. It's very difficult for anyone to identify and articulate their values in the abstract, but visualisation techniques can be helpful to make it all a bit more concrete. Ask your participants to imagine themselves in the future – perhaps at their own retirement party, or if your clients are younger, perhaps at the leaving-do from their first job. Ask them to imagine their boss getting up to make a speech about them, and then get them to think about what they would want their boss to say. What sort of achievements or impact do they want to be remembered for? How would they want people to describe them after they finish work?

The de-brief: Once you have finished the activities, you need to spend some time working out what this all means to your client. What values have they identified? What matters to them? What, for them, constitutes a successful first job or a successful career? And what is next for them? What can they do now to work towards this?

Key takeaways

Career success has three elements which are distinct but linked.

Objective career success is linked to salary and influence.

Subjective career success is a measure of how you feel about what you have achieved.

Job satisfaction is a combination of pleasure and meaning.

Job satisfaction and subjective career success lead to people being more objectively successful.

The model can be used to help clients work out what career success looks like for them.

Holland's RIASEC Hexagon

Introduction

This idea that underpins this model is all about matching people with jobs. This notion stems right back to Frank Parsons – the father of career guidance – who in 1909 articulated the common-sense view that we should be looking for jobs or careers to which we are well suited to. Parsons' idea has spawned a number of different theories over the years, but John Holland's theory of career interests, developed in the US in the 1950s, is undoubtedly the most widely known and most influential.

We can think about this idea of a good match from different angles. The academic literature talks about finding a fit between the person and their environment, organisation and job; but we can also think about different facets of ourselves and look for a job that aligns with our values, our skills, our practical requirements or our sense of identity. These are all important, and some of them we cover elsewhere in the book. But what we are looking at in this model is what John Holland calls vocational personality types, or what you might think of as career interests.

Holland's starting point is that people are likely to be happiest at work when there is a good match between their personality or interests and their role. Back in the 1950s, he conducted large-scale studies that seemed to show that people who were thriving in particular jobs had similar vocational personalities, and plenty of studies since then support the idea that a good fit brings benefits to the individual and the organisation.

Holland identified six different vocational personality types. which are known by the acronym RIASEC:

- Realistic
- Investigative
- Artistic
- Social
- Enterprising
- Conventional

They are placed in this order around a hexagon. The order is quite specific – similar personality types are adjacent to each other and different types are opposite each other.

Q Critical viewpoint

Holland comes in for a lot of criticism in the more contemporary career literature. The problems with his approach, according to his critics, are that it assumes that people and jobs are both stable and that career choices are things that are made once – during or after school – that we stick with all our working lives. Those assumptions clearly would be problematic. People's interests and values change and develop, jobs evolve and people make career choices many times throughout their lifetime. We know that. But although Holland devised his theory based on some outdated assumptions, I think that the idea of finding a job that suits you is a good one. We just need to keep in mind (and remind our clients) that jobs and people change and develop over time, and a matching exercise like this one will only ever show a snapshot of how things are at one particular point in time.

The RIASEC Hexagon

Here are Holland's definitions of the six types. Perhaps you can recognise yourself in one or two of them?

Realistic: conforming, frank, genuine, hard-headed, materialistic, persistent, practical, self-effacing, inflexible, thrifty. Realistic types usually have mechanical abilities and enjoy working with things. They will often excel in hands-on roles and tend to be good at fixing things. They can enjoy work that is physically active and involves using tools.

Investigative: intellectual, introspective thinkers who are inquisitive, curious and methodical. Investigative types enjoy academic pursuits and like to understand things. They often enjoy working with facts and finding out the truth and can excel in scientific arenas.

Artistic: creative, intuitive, expressive with a strong imagination and an enjoyment of abstract thoughts and ideas. Artistic people enjoy using their imagination and can be creative both intellectually and aesthetically.

Social: kind, caring, empathic and warm. Social types enjoy being with and analysing people. They like to help people solve their problems and are interested in how relationships work and how people interact. They are often found in caring professions, such as social work, counselling and teaching, but can excel in any role which relies on strong relationships.

Enterprising: energetic, sociable, lively, ambitious risk-takers. Enterprising types like to influence, persuade, lead and direct. They often have strong

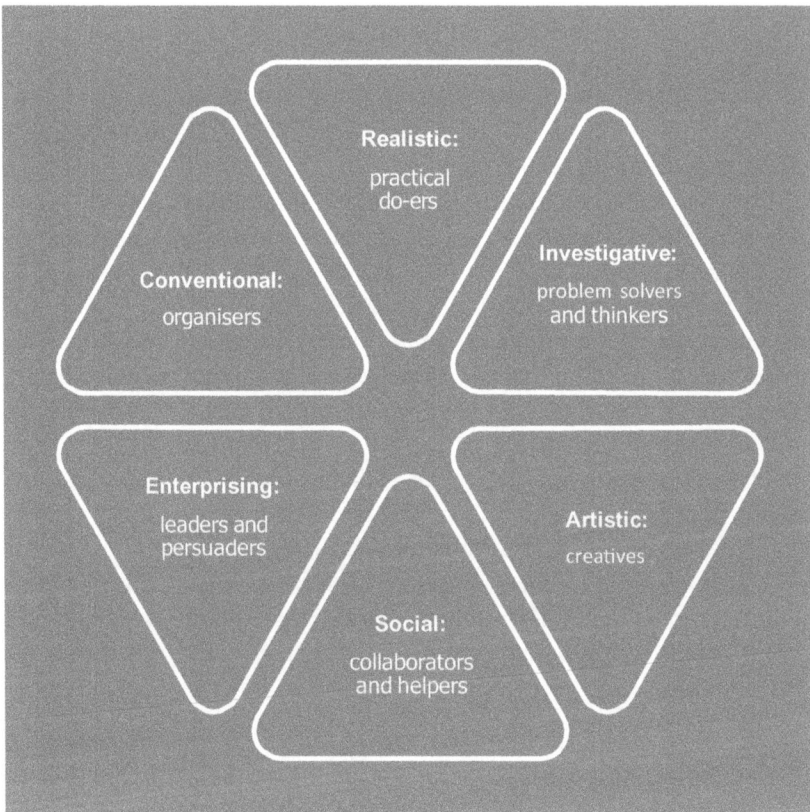

Figure 10.2 Holland's RIASEC Hexagon.

leadership skills and enjoy public speaking. Their ability to persuade and influence means that they can enjoy working in highly political environments and can excel in sales roles.

Conventional: detail-oriented completer-finishers. Conventional types enjoy order and routines and prefer working in a more predictable way, where expectations and standards are clear. They are likely to enjoy work that involves organisation and are often found in work that focuses on things and systems, rather than data and people.

People can usually be categorised as having one dominant personality and then one or two less dominant characteristics. These less dominant characteristics are typically found on either side of the dominant one on the hexagon. So, if you are most clearly a *social* type, you are quite likely to be *artistic* or *enterprising*, and less likely to be *realistic*.

The RIASEC Hexagon in practice

This tool may be most useful when working with clients who are at an early stage in their career thinking and perhaps haven't spent much time reflecting on themselves and what they want in a job. It can be a useful starting point for a conversation, although I think there are some useful caveats to bear in mind. First, it's important to remember, and to remind your client, that career interests are only one aspect of what is important in a career (strengths, values, practicalities and such like all play their part). Secondly, these things are fluid. Career interests change, and the nature of jobs will change too, so these are not permanent or fixed badges of identity.

1) As a self-awareness tool. The model can be used as a self-awareness tool to help clients start to think about themselves in the workplace. You can either just present your clients with these kinds of brief descriptions of the six types or have a look online for some of the many free online tests. This can be a useful starting point for the kinds of things that a client might find particularly interesting in a role.

2) To generate job ideas. RIASEC job lists can be a starting point for a conversation about specific job ideas for clients. You can find lists that link the RIASEC codes to particular jobs online. Invite your client to look through the list and think about which job ideas appeal to them, and what they find attractive in those roles. This approach works really well to give your clients a starting point, with some tangible job ideas that are going to be reasonably relevant. But of course, do emphasise to your client that this is a list to start them thinking about what they want from a job, not a definitive list of the occupations that will suit them.

3) To reflect on the career choice process. Paradoxically, one of the problems with this theory is that it is so intuitive. It seems so obvious that this is how people should make career choices that people (clients and also some of our other stakeholders) sometimes don't look beyond it to understand the complexities of career decisions. One way you could use this, perhaps in a career education setting, is as a comparison. You could, for example, show this model alongside some more complex theories such as Patton and McMahon's systems framework (Chapter 6) or Lent, Brown and Hackett's Social Cognitive Career Theory (Chapter 9) to explore different ideas of career choice. Ask your clients then to think about the different approaches to see which they feel is most accurate, or most useful.

RIASEC WITH PHD RESEARCHERS

Sarah Blackford

I remember doing a workshop years and years ago for people who didn't have a clue about what they wanted to do. There was a real mix of people in the room from humanities, social sciences, the sciences and so on. And I just felt that there was nothing to really hang it on. It was a bit wishy-washy. I thought we need a framework. And I turned to Holland's RIASEC model.

I thought in some way it would help people focus in on particular areas of work that might be of interest to them or particular skills that they use that are more interesting than others.

It's a very straightforward model that I've developed over the years. I use Holland's hexagon, but I've changed a couple of the descriptors. So instead of *realistic*, I've got *functional* and instead of *conventional*, I've got *management* because I thought that these terms were more understandable. I show the hexagon and explain the six types, and then I ask my clients, my students, my postdocs, whoever they are, either in a group or individually, to identify the kind of skills that they use while they're working, doing their research or outside of their research in their lives, doing whatever they do. And then we try to categorise their tasks or skills into the various areas that are identified on the hexagon to give them an idea that, for example, perhaps they are doing a lot of functional work at the moment, but actually, they might really prefer a bit more of the social side, or perhaps they're doing a lot of artistic stuff, and they feel that they are not doing enough enterprising stuff.

It's all about self-awareness. It's not trying to match people up to particular jobs; it's more about raising awareness. And I think if it's used in the right way, Holland's model is still relevant.

I mainly use this in group sessions. People sit together and just talk about the tasks that they do, and they all just put them onto post-it notes and sort of chuck them into the middle. We do this brainstorm, and they see what everyone else is doing and maybe think, oh, look at what that person is doing. Maybe they've forgotten about things that they do. When they categorise their skills or tasks according to the RIASEC types, it helps to raise their self-awareness and think about what kind of jobs or roles would allow them to use the skills that they enjoy.

I am generally explicit with my clients that this exercise is based on a theory by John Holland. I work with academic types, and I think they like to know where everything's coming from. I don't usually tell them about the theory straight away, but I get them to do the exercise first and then explain the theory.

Key takeaways

People are likely to be happiest and most productive when there is a good match between the person and their environment.

Holland identified six vocational personality types described as RIASEC: Realistic, Investigative, Artistic, Social, Enterprising and Conventional.

Each of us is likely to be drawn to two or three of these types.

There are particular jobs that are thought to suit people with different vocational personality types.

This approach is useful as a starting point for a conversation and to boost self-awareness and generate job ideas.

Career Self-Determination Theory

Introduction

There are two theories I'm incorporating here. The original theory was developed by two American psychologists, Ryan and Deci (pronounced Dee-See), in the mid-1980s. It's a theory of motivation, and I find it useful in all sorts of settings to understand why my clients are not feeling very driven. It's a theory of psychological needs: in the way that we all have physical needs to let our bodies survive and thrive (water, shelter, safety etc.), we also have psychological needs which are required to ensure that our minds can survive and thrive and that our wellbeing doesn't suffer.

Self-Determination Theory identifies three specific psychological needs:

Relatedness: We all have a need to feel that we are relating to people, that there are people in our lives who share our worldview, whose values align with ours, who are working towards the same goals, who care about us and who we care about. Without connections, we struggle in all areas of our lives.

Competence: We need to feel that we have some capacity to succeed in what we are doing. If we feel incompetent and, crucially, if we feel that we aren't improving or developing, then we are going to lose enthusiasm altogether and are likely to withdraw.

Autonomy: Finally, we need to feel at some level that we have some control over our lives, whether that is what and how we do things, or when and where we do them. Having some sense of choice makes us far more motivated to work hard and overcome barriers.

Together these three psychological needs lead to intrinsic motivation. You feel *intrinsic* motivation when you do something just because you want to do it – when you actually enjoy the work itself. This contrasts with *extrinsic* motivation, which motivates you to do something because it's going to lead to a desirable goal – for example if you are working simply for the pay packet at the end of the week. Intrinsic motivation is generally much more powerful.

You may be able to think of some times in your career or life more generally when you lacked motivation – I wonder whether you can trace any of your lack of motivation back to one of those three psychological needs?

Charles Chen has adapted the original theory to make it even more relevant to a career context, and his Career Self-Determination Theory is the second theory we are looking at here.

Career Self-Determination Theory
The three elements of Career Self-Determination Theory ask questions to determine whether your career is meeting your psychological needs.

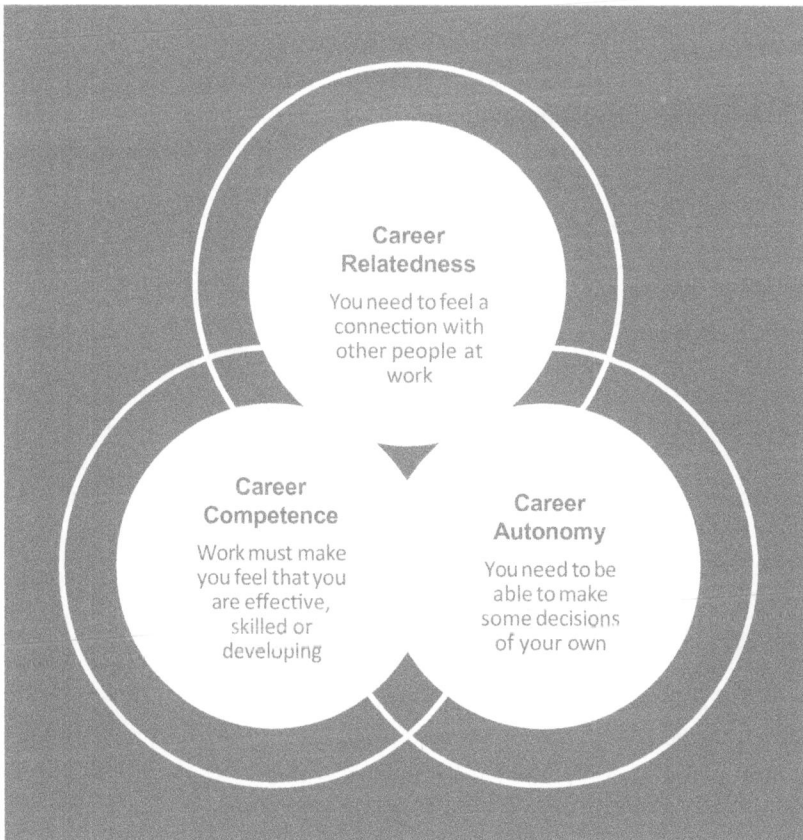

Figure 10.3 Chen's Career Self-Determination Theory.

Career Relatedness: This is the degree to which your career allows or facilitates positive relationships. This could be applied within work – do you feel connected with at least some of the people you work with? It could be colleagues, clients, customers or other stakeholders, and the relatedness could take different forms – friendship, office banter, shared values or goals, or close working relationships. But it can also be applied to relationships outside work – asking whether your work allows you to, for example, be the parent, the partner, the daughter or the friend that you want to be.

Career Competence: This relates to feeling able to do your job. It could reflect the degree to which you are suited to the role – do you have the strengths, attributes and experience to do your job well? It could be linked to the support or guidance you get at work – are you clear about what you should be doing, do you feel supported to do it and are you given the feedback and training you need to improve? It could also be to do with resources – have you got the time and equipment you need to do your job well enough?

Career Autonomy: This has two distinct aspects. First, there is autonomy within the job. Are you able to make some choices within your job – do you have at least some scope to choose what you focus on, how you work or when and where you get things done? Having this kind of control within the job is important, but it's also important to feel that you have some choice about the job you have or the organisation you work for. Do you feel that you made a choice to work in this particular role? And do you feel that you have to stay? Or do you feel that you chose to work in that organisation and that you are staying because you want to, rather than because you have no other options?

Career Self-Determination Theory in practice

As a framework for reflection: I find these two theories really useful as frameworks to help clients reflect on things in the past that haven't gone well for them. When clients tell their stories about previous jobs that haven't worked out, or a current job that feels unmotivating, listen out for comments about relatedness, autonomy or competence. There are often issues around a misalignment of values (that can be relatedness), a micro-managing boss (autonomy) or a system that won't allow them to work effectively (competence).

In these situations, you can share the theory with your client explicitly, inviting them to reflect on whether it resonates with their experience. For a client, finding out that what they have experienced is the subject of a theory can be enormously validating. A negative experience can be a difficult thing to come to terms with, and people often feel it is their fault. Finding out that, actually, their employer was restricting one of their three fundamental psychological needs highlights that the problem wasn't with them, and this can give them renewed confidence.

To analyse job ideas: One of the nicest challenges that our clients can face is having too many options to choose from. Self-Determination Theory can help clients assess different options to think about which might suit them best. Invite your client to give each job option a score of 1–10, based on their best guess as to how well it will meet their needs for autonomy, relatedness and competence. Ask them to think hard about what they have based this on, and then invite them to think about the implications.

Key takeaways

In the way that we have physical needs that must be met to allow our bodies to survive and thrive, we also have psychological needs to ensure that our minds survive and thrive.

The three key psychological needs are relatedness, competence and autonomy.

If we are in jobs that don't allow us to feel connected to others, where we don't feel we are working effectively and where we feel we have no control, we won't be motivated or fulfilled.

This framework of psychological needs can help clients understand why jobs didn't work out for them in the past and judge whether future jobs are likely to suit them.

Chapter 11
Theories to help explain the experiences of marginalised groups

Overview

There have been criticisms over the years that most career theories are tailored to white, middle-class men. More recently, the career research community has started to develop theories that focus on other groups of people and in this chapter we look at three such theories:

- *The Psychology of Working Theory* that explains some of the career experiences of people who are marginalised by society and who have limited economic resources.
- *The Kaleidoscope Career Model,* which examines women's motivations across their working lives.
- *The Cultural Preparation Process Model* that unpicks the influence of culture on our understanding and approach to work and career.

A core part of the motivation of many career professionals is to help make the working world a better place. I think we manage to do this in all sorts of different ways, but one particular strategy is through the idea of social justice – trying to make the working world fairer, allowing people to lead the lives they want to and have the careers they want to, regardless of their starting point in life. We often see clients who haven't had the advantage of certain types of privilege, and we are all aware of the limits that this can place on their ambitions, aspirations, expectations, opportunities and reality. If there is anything that we can do to try and help level the playing field, then that is time well spent.

Historically, career theories were based on the career paths of white, Western, middle-class, able-bodied, neurotypical men. Anyone who fell outside that narrow demographic group was implicitly considered to have a non-standard, sub-standard or deviant career path. More recently, the academic field has started to realise that the world of work will be better for accommodating and capitalising on the strengths of all kinds of members of society, and that different theories need to be developed to encompass everyone's experiences. A number of new theories have been developed, and some of the older theories have been adapted to accommodate or encompass particular client groups. In this chapter I want to introduce three theories that are explicitly focused on groups of people who are not white, Western, middle-class men. The first is Blustein's *Psychology of Working Theory*, which looks at the career paths of marginalised people and highlights the impact that both marginalisation and low economic resources can have on people's sense of choice over their work and their chances of finding good jobs. The second theory is Mainiero and Sullivan's *Kaleidoscope Career Model*, which describes the career paths of women throughout their lives. Finally, Arulmani's *Cultural Preparation Process Model* focuses on the influence of cultures on people's conceptualisations of work and career.

The Psychology of Working Theory

Introduction

One assumption implicit within the traditional focus on those who have certain levels of privilege, is that people have some degree of choice and some sense of autonomy over their career paths — a belief that they do genuinely have a choice about what they do. The Psychology of Working Theory (PWT) focuses on a different group of people — those who are marginalised by society and who have limited economic resources behind them. PWT aims to explain the impact that marginalisation and low pay have on people's choice, and in doing so, offers us a good starting point for trying to change things.

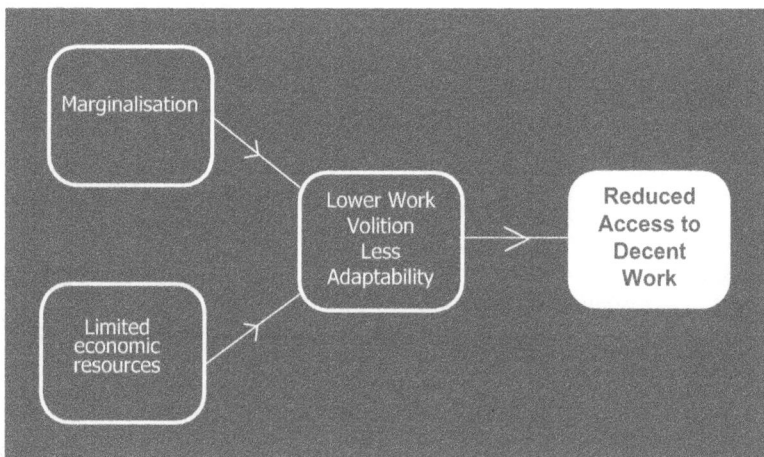

Figure 11.1 Blustein's Psychology of Working Theory.

At the heart of the theory is the notion of decent work as a human right and a core goal of career practice. Blustein and his colleagues define *decent work* in quite a technical way, but it's really the common-sense idea that everyone should be paid a decent wage, should not be asked to work unreasonable hours and that we all have the right to feel safe at work. There are, unfortunately, plenty of people both across the world and here in the UK who don't have access to decent work, and the research is clear that people who have limited financial resources and who are marginalised by society are less likely to be in decent jobs.

PWT identifies two key barriers to decent work: limited work volition and low levels of career adaptability. Work volition is the belief that you have some degree of choice over which job you do. If you have a low level of work volition, then you believe that you have no option other than to take a particular job, or stick with the one you've got, even if it's awful. You might feel that no one else would employ you, that there simply aren't any other roles you could possibly get or that it wouldn't be worth the risk of leaving for fear of finding yourself in an even worse position.

You can see that this might link with decent work: people who have a strong sense of work volition – people who believe that they have other options – would simply not put up with a job that didn't pay reasonably, or where they didn't feel safe. They would either negotiate to improve their conditions or just walk out, confident that they would be able to find something else. By contrast, people with low levels of work volition feel that there are no other options for them, so they won't try to change things.

You can also see how a low level of work volition might be associated with marginalisation and a lack of economic resources. Feeling marginalised by society could lead you to believe that there just aren't that many employers who would want you, and having limited economic resources to fall back on could make you feel that you couldn't afford not to work; demanding better conditions might lead to you being fired, or could make your working conditions even worse, and this might not be a risk you feel that you could take.

The second barrier to decent work is a low level of career adaptability. According to PWT, career adaptability can make us feel that we are in control – that we have a high level of work volition. The more career adaptable we are, the more confident we will feel that we are able to make choices. We came across career adaptability in Chapter 8 (so do have a look at the ideas for practice on page 75), but just to remind you, this refers to the degree to which an individual can anticipate and respond to the changing demands of the workplace. Career adaptability in PWT draws from Savickas and Porfeli's four Cs model, conceptualising career adaptability as made up of:

- Career concern – the level of interest, engagement and investment someone puts into their career development.

- Career curiosity – the desire to explore new experiences, find information and opportunities for learning.

- Career confidence – an individual's belief in their own ability to do well at work.

- Career control – the sense of agency and autonomy in career development.

The Psychology of Working Theory in practice

As with many of the theories in this book, this one won't apply to all of your clients. But if you are working with someone who seems to feel that their choices are unrealistically limited, or who might be prepared to put up with poor working conditions for fear of being out of work altogether, then here are some ideas for practice.

1) *Recognise your clients' experiences.* Career professionals can offer an important service by hearing and seeing clients. People who feel marginalised and feel that they don't have much control or agency over their careers can very often feel overlooked. Career professionals can boost their clients' wellbeing and sense of self-esteem by listening and acknowledging their experiences.

2) *Foster critical consciousness.* This is a term that is widely used in the PWT literature, and it's all about raising our clients' awareness of their situation and encouraging them to reflect on the barriers that society has imposed on them. The research shows that if we can manage this, it genuinely helps clients to feel a greater sense of control over their career paths, and to believe that there are more options out there for them. Sharing details of the model explicitly with clients can help with this. You might want to just focus on the notion of decent work – simply telling your clients that their working conditions fall short of the basic human right can encourage your client to see that it's not them who is at fault. This can help to empower them to try to make a change.

3) *Boost self-efficacy.* We talked in more detail in Chapter 7 about ways to boost self-efficacy, and it is striking how often this concept seems to come up in these career theories. The most direct route to increased self-efficacy is what they term 'mastery experiences' – doing things well. Giving clients the chance to practice things could really make them feel more confident. So you might want to offer them the chance to role-play a negotiation with their boss or a job interview. Vicarious learning (learning from watching others) can work really well too, so try to get hold of some success stories of similar clients, or try to encourage your client to think about

people they know, in a similar situation, who have managed to make a positive move.

Key takeaways

The Psychology of Working Theory focuses on the career paths of people who are marginalised in society and who have limited economic resources.

It centres around the importance of 'decent work' where we are paid appropriately, where we work reasonable hours and where we feel safe. It shows that people who are marginalised and lack economic resources are less likely to find decent work.

Some of this is explained by a lack of work volition – the feeling that you are in control of your own career choices.

Career support can help clients understand the systemic challenges they face and can encourage them to feel more empowered.

The Kaleidoscope Career Model

Introduction

The authors of this theory were very struck that the traditional career theories described and explained the career paths of men. They were aware that women often made different kinds of choices in their careers but felt that traditional career theories conceptualised these different career paths as being exceptional, and as inferior to the traditional male paths. In particular, Mainiero and Sullivan seemed to get really cross about one particular narrative which described the 'opt-out revolution', which puts women's lack of representation in C-suite roles down, in large part, to women's lack of ambition.

Mainiero and Sullivan wanted to explore what was really going on, so they conducted an enormous study of men's and women's career paths and motivations across the career span, and on the back of that developed a model.

The model focuses on motivation or drivers for career decisions across the lifespan. The authors suggest that for all of us – men and women – there are three key career drivers which influence our choices throughout our careers: Authenticity, Balance and Challenge.

Authenticity: The drive for authenticity is all about wanting a job or organisation where you feel that you can genuinely be yourself; an organisation whose

121

values align with your own, and a job that allows you to work towards something that you feel matters and where your work identity feels like a reasonable reflection of who you really are.

Balance: A job in which you have balance is one that allows you to be the person that you want to be outside working hours. This might be a job where the hours are limited or flexible in some way, to give you the time to do whatever you want to do outside working hours, or just one that enables you to switch off mentally when you aren't at work. A balanced job could allow you to fulfil other roles in your life, for example, being the mother or father that you want to be, or allowing you to spend the time you need with your parents. It might also allow you the time to pursue a side hustle or a hobby.

Challenge: This driver is about the desire for professional development and success – your challenge driver pushes you to learn more, develop new knowledge and skill and to work hard towards promotions or pay raises.

The Kaleidoscope Career Model (KCM) proposes that all three of these drivers are usually present in all of us throughout our whole career path. This makes sense to me – I mean, which of us doesn't want to feel that we are in jobs that allow us to be authentic, to develop and to have time to devote to the things that matter outside work? But the strength of each of the drivers waxes and wanes throughout our lives, and one driver might take centre stage during one phase of our career, with the other two fading a little bit into the background. The model also indicates that the typical pattern is different for men and women.

In Figure 11.2, you can see the typical pattern for women and men.

Critical viewpoint

The authors describe these career paths as typical, not universal – they are quite aware that the model won't account for everyone. There are plenty of women who follow the 'typical' male path and vice versa. You will also note that it doesn't account for non-binary or genderfluid people at all, so it definitely doesn't apply to everyone! Another implicit assumption in the model that you might also want to question, is whether all of our clients actually have the freedom to follow their drivers in this way. Some of our clients, for example, might be desperately keen on having more of a balance, but perhaps their financial circumstances mean that this is just not possible. This idea was explored in the Psychology of Working Theory earlier in the chapter.

The model clearly doesn't apply to everyone, which you could argue makes it flawed. But that doesn't mean that it isn't useful – it just means that you need to pick and choose when you use it and how you describe it.

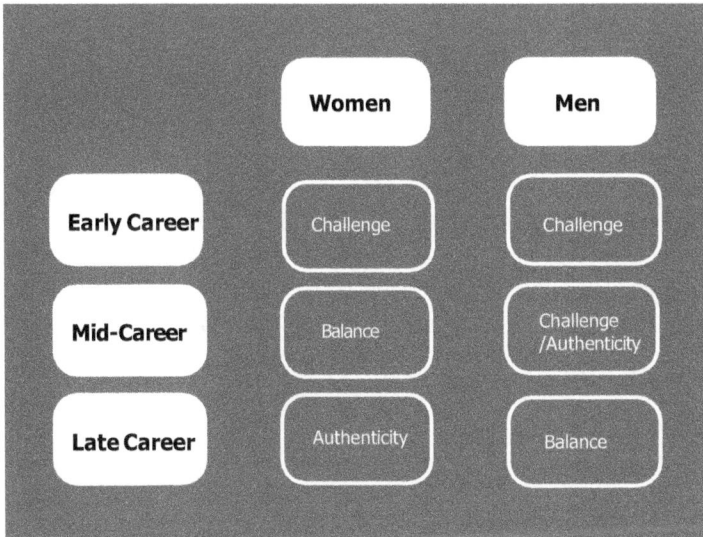

Figure 11.2 Sullivan and Mainiero's Kaleidoscope Career Model.

Early Career: During their early careers it is common for both women and men to be predominantly driven by challenge. This doesn't mean that authenticity and balance aren't important, but the drive for challenge is often the dominant one. Throughout these early years, women and men are drawn to jobs where they feel that they are growing professionally: learning new skills, building networks, soaking up new knowledge and developing expertise. During this phase, people seek new opportunities and work towards pay raises and promotions.

Mid-Career: During the mid-career stage, men and women's typical patterns start to diverge. Men often continue to be driven by challenge, still striving towards salary and seniority and working hard to achieve them. For some, this may be tied to fatherhood, and some men may feel societal or family pressure to be a strong breadwinner. At this stage, authenticity can start to make its presence felt too as men perhaps become more aware of what matters to them and want to carve out a career that aligns with who they really are. Women at this stage can become more driven to find a balance within their career — looking for work that allows them to be the person they want to be outside the office. This can often be linked to motherhood, as women look for jobs that offer them the flexibility they need to be the mother they want to be. But research seems to indicate that child-free women are also keen on balance at this life stage — often choosing to work part-time to pursue hobbies or just to live a more balanced life.

Late Career: Men, during their late career, can often start to feel that they want more balance in their lives. Perhaps they feel that they have been working hard for decades and feel that it's time to take their foot off the gas.

At this stage, they might choose to spend a bit more time on their leisure interests, or with their grandchildren or might take on other kinds of roles, getting involved in volunteering or consultancy work where they can pass down some of their lifetime of expertise.

Women at this stage often start to pursue authenticity. Some women in their later career stage might feel that they are free from other obligations. Perhaps their children have now left home, or at least need less hands-on care. Perhaps their parents have sadly passed away, leaving them more time to themselves. Both these changes can also mean that women sometimes feel the desire to find a new identity, or a new way to find meaning. And so they channel this into work, looking for a role that allows them to bring their whole selves to work and to find something that aligns with their values, where they feel that they can make a meaningful contribution.

The 'kaleidoscope' of the model relates to a children's toy – I don't know whether you had one of these in your own childhood? A kaleidoscope looks a bit like a telescope but it is filled with coloured mosaic tiles and angled mirrors that make brightly coloured patterns that change when you turn it around. The tiles move around very easily, and the mirrors mean that even a slight movement in one of the mosaic tiles causes the whole image to change substantially. This, according to Mainiero and Sullivan, is a metaphor for what happens in women's careers: when something in one part of their lives changes, this has a knock-on impact on everything else. Most often, this one thing is 'relational' – that is, linked to family – which could be becoming a mother, caring for parents or moving for a spouse's job. Any one of these changes, although not directly linked to the woman's job, will usually have a significant knock-on impact on the way she works and the way she sees her career at that stage in life.

The KCM in practice

I mentioned above that the model is not meant to explain everyone's career paths, but if you are working with mid or late career women, I'm sure you will recognise the pattern.

Building self-confidence. One thing that we know about women is that they often suffer from low confidence. This holds true for an awful lot of women throughout much of their lives, but you can really see it with women who have changed their working patterns to accommodate their families during their mid-career years. These women can really struggle to imagine how society or employers will see value in them and can question what they have to contribute. One thing that exacerbates this sense of self-doubt is that our cultural expectations of a 'career' are built on the traditional male model: when we think of a typical 'successful' career path, it's one that is fairly linear, involving step-by-step promotions and pay raises, and when we think of a typical 'successful' career person, they have generally devoted themselves to their work throughout their lives. Women who have not pursued the traditional male path – those who have decided to focus on their families or on other priorities – can feel that they have in some way let themselves down, perhaps failing to capitalise on their education or their early career success, and can often feel almost embarrassed by the choices they have made. The phrase '*just a stay-at-home mum*' or '*just a housewife*' comes up a lot in conversations with this group of clients, and that word '*just*' conveys a lot about how the women feel about themselves and how society sees them. Sharing the details of the model explicitly with this group can show them that they are not alone, and can illustrate that rather than having made poor decisions and chosen a less impressive path, their choices have been positive and proactive. It can make the point that this well-trodden career path for women isn't inferior to that more commonly seen in men; it's just different. This can be enormously validating for women.

To develop self-awareness: The ABC model looks at three key career drivers – Authenticity, Balance and Challenge. These drivers can be used as a framework to help clients consider their own motivations and weigh the relative importance of the three. They could then consider any potential job opportunities and assess the degree to which the jobs are likely to meet their needs. This self-awareness exercise could be used at any stage of a client's career but might be particularly interesting during mid or late career when the clients can think not just about where they are now, but how their motivation has changed over the years.

THE KCM WITH CAREER CHANGERS

Penny Taylor

The KCM is one of my favourite career models – the ABC model of the drivers is really easy to remember, and it really resonates with so many of my clients. I work as a career coach, and I do a lot of work with women in mid and late career, and a lot of them are really low in confidence. I often use it with this client group.

Last week I was working with a client from this group, in her early 50s. She had recently resigned from a job that she was really not enjoying and wanted some help planning the next stage in her career. She was in PR. She had built quite a successful career for herself in health PR in her 20s and 30s but then took some time off paid work altogether when her children were little, and for the last 10 years or so, had worked part-time in a local PR firm. She hadn't enjoyed this role for some time and said that she had got to an age where she decided that life was just too short to be doing something you don't really like. So she resigned to give herself some time to think about what she wanted next.

At this point, the three phases of the KCM were really ringing bells. To me, this was a textbook example of someone who started mostly driven by *challenge*, looked for *balance* to allow her to be the mother she wanted to be in her mid-years, and was now looking for some *authenticity*. I tried out the language of the KCM at this point and said something like, 'It sounds as though you are looking for a job now where you feel authentic – where you can do something that really matters to you at work', and this really seemed to resonate with her. I think this made her feel that I genuinely understood where she was coming from, and actually, I think it also seemed to help her crystallise for herself what she meant. So I felt that was useful.

And then later she seemed to be looking around for some term to describe her choices – she seemed to want a label that allowed her to join a tribe of women who had made similar career choices. I offered the term 'opt-out revolution', and she seemed to really like it – not so much the meaning of the term itself, but the very fact that there was a term. I thought I'd try the model itself and so described the three stages briefly to her, and she seemed really pleased with it. It seemed to make her feel like she was part of a group – women who had all looked for challenge and then balance and who were now looking for authenticity. And she seemed almost proud of herself, that she had followed a Kaleidoscopic career. She sort of sat up a bit taller, and I felt that she was more accepting, maybe even more proud, of her own decisions.

Key takeaways

The Kaleidoscope Career Model focuses specifically on the career paths of women. It suggests that there are three key career drivers that are present in us all throughout our career paths:

- *Authenticity* is the desire to be able to feel yourself in your job.
- *Balance* is the desire to have a job that allows you to have the life you want beyond the workplace.
- *Challenge* is the drive to grow, develop and become more senior and influential.

Women often follow a career path in which Challenge dominates in their early career, Balance in their mid-career years, and Authenticity in their late career.

The Cultural Preparation Process Model

Introduction

This model explains how culture influences our understanding of work and career. It can be useful in helping us to understand clients who have been influenced by two different cultures (e.g. migrants who have influences from the country they were born in and the country they now live in), and it's particularly important for us as career professionals when we are working with clients whose cultural influences are different from our own.

The model starts with an assumption that everything we know, the way we view the world, how we behave, our values and our expectations about life, are all based in large part on our context – where we grew up, who we learnt from, what we saw, what we heard and what we did. Our context determines how we understand the world, how we behave and what we believe. It has a lot in common with Bill Law's idea of Community Interaction (Chapter 6) but goes further, showing that our community and culture have shaped not just how we see things, but our actual reality – what we believe is true.

This idea of different truths and realities could have quite an impact on any of us working with clients from cultures that are different from our own. The model also reminds us that work itself is a cultural construct – the way we see work, and our understanding of the notions of a 'good job' or a 'good career' are all a product of the culture in which we grew up and now live.

Overview

The approach rests on four constructs:

Cultural learning: We are evolved to learn about our environment, and culture actually structures the way we learn. Without even consciously realising it, we learn about the world through the lens of our culture. Our understanding of what the world is and how it works is taught to us as we watch and listen to the people around us.

Enculturation: This understanding of the world and how it works is our reality. We assume that it is true, accurate and correct. Work is one aspect of the world we absorb from our culture, and work becomes what our culture tells us it is – individualistic cultures conceptualise work as an individual badge of identity and pride. Collectivist cultures see it as a reflection of the family or community.

Cultural preparation status equilibrium: This equilibrium describes the way that our culturally derived understanding of the world just seems to make sense – that's just how it is and how we do it, and how we see it. It shapes our expectations and assumptions about how we work, why we work and what we do.

127

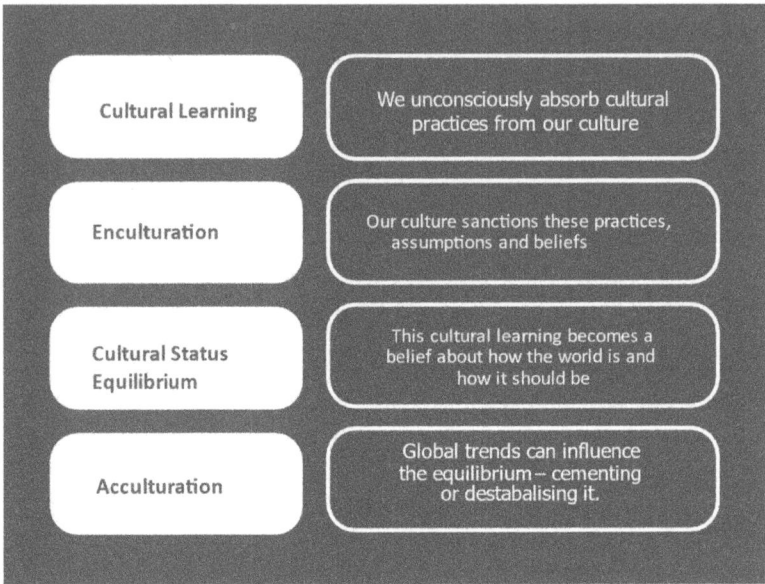

Figure 11.3 Arulmani's Cultural Preparation Process Model.

Acculturation: This is all about the bigger picture – the global trends and the macro-conditions that have an impact on us. These influences include political upheavals, wars, natural disasters or technological breakthroughs – all factors beyond the control of the individual and their culture. These can either cement the equilibrium reached in the previous point, or destabilise it.

The Cultural Preparation Process Model in practice
The whole point of the CPPM is to encourage us to be more culturally sensitive in our career conversations. Arulmani talks about the importance of *culture concordant interventions,* suggesting that we should make sure that the career interventions we run are designed to suit our clients. Research backs this up, supporting the principle that career interventions that are adapted to the particular culture of the client are more effective.

Arulmani makes a number of suggestions for us to consider, aimed at encouraging us to recognise that almost everything we believe is based on our own enculturation. Our understanding of what a career is, what a good career is, how to make good decisions, how to assess someone, what a skill is and pretty much everything else is all based on our own cultural embeddedness. We see these things as objective truths, but they aren't; they are subjective cultural assumptions. If we can start to see them as such, we will then be open to the idea that our clients might see them differently, and we can meet our clients where they are, rather than where we are.

This understanding will underpin everything that we do within our careers interventions, but highlight three key things that we should think about:

Collectivist decision-making: The UK and most Western cultures are individualistic. In career planning terms, this means that we assume that an individual will and should make a career decision that is going to suit them and allow them to fulfil their own ambitions and live the life they want to live. Other cultures are collectivist, which means that people see themselves as one part of a bigger collective – one part of their family or their community – and as such must make a career decision that will suit their family and allow them to contribute to the family's ambitions and futures. A culturally sensitive career intervention, then, would involve us accepting that clients might be making decisions that are not in their own best interests but in the best interests of their community or family. And it might involve actually inviting their family members to be involved in their interventions, either inviting our clients to bring their family members along to the careers intervention if they want to or offering some written materials or notes that are explicitly aimed at helping our clients to share the information that we discuss with their family.

Narrative approaches: Every culture has its own set of culturally anchored symbols. A career intervention that can incorporate the client's own cultural symbols will be more likely to be effective. One type of symbol that is present in almost every culture is storytelling, which is a vehicle for making sense of a dilemma through the lens of other cultural symbols. Using storytelling as a tool in career development can really allow our clients to apply their own cultural lens to their own career dilemmas and can help us as career professionals understand their perspective more empathically.

Assessments: Finally, a CPPM approach suggests that we should think about how we assess our clients. The way we think about assessing people is culturally embedded. In some cultures, only quantitative measures hold much sway. In others, only qualitative methods are credible. The CPPM suggests that assessments that are mixed – incorporating qualitative and quantitative methods – appeal to a wide range of cultures. But it also makes sense to offer your client a choice. For example, if you wanted to help your client to raise their self-awareness and generate job ideas, you could offer your clients the choice of some kind of quantitative online matching assessment tool or a strengths exercise using cards as a more qualitative approach. Your client could then pick the one that, as far as they are concerned, has the most credibility.

Key takeaways

Our culture shapes not just what we know about, but how we see reality and what we believe is true. It does this through four processes:

- Cultural learning explains that we learn about the world by observing and listening to the people around us.

- Enculturation: We start to see these behaviours, assumptions, expectations and social norms as correct, and we enact them ourselves.

- Cultural status equilibrium is the point where these cultural learnings get so embedded that they become part of our reality.

- Acculturation: This acknowledges that events beyond our immediate culture, such as geo-political events, natural disasters and emerging technologies, have an impact.

The important thing for us to remember as career professionals is that people who have grown up in a different culture from our own have a different reality. Our realities are all culturally determined, and we must remember that something we believe to be true may simply not be true for one of our clients. Using a storytelling approach can help us understand our client's reality.

Chapter 12
Theories to boost employability

Overview

Some people seem to be better at getting and keeping jobs than others.

There are certain characteristics that can help, and in this chapter, we're going to look at three models that identify these qualities:

- *The Intelligent Career Framework*
- *Psychological Capital*
- *The Model of Career Resources*

Helping your clients work on these attributes will boost their chances of getting and excelling in the roles they want.

The three models in this chapter are all about employability. Each describes a set of attributes we need to develop in order to get the jobs we want, to keep them, and to carry on getting and keeping jobs throughout our lives. The three models are: Arthur and Filippi's Intelligent Career Framework, Luthans' model of Psychological Capital, and Fugate, Ashforth and Kinicki's Psycho-Social model of employability. There are considerable overlaps between these models, but I think that's quite reassuring – it gives me some confidence that the models are probably all covering the right qualities, even if each model has a slightly different focus. You can just pick the one that resonates best with you and your clients.

The ideas in the models can be useful with clients of all ages and stages – and I hope you will also be able to use them to think about your own employability and career planning as we go through.

The Intelligent Career Framework

Introduction

The Intelligent Career Framework was designed to help us navigate career paths in the contemporary working world. Work in the 21st century is characterised by rapid change and more fluid career paths, which often encompass moves, shifts, twists and turns. We need to develop the right skills to help us thrive in this unstable and unpredictable labour market, and the Intelligent Career Framework (ICF) is a useful starting point for this.

According to the ICF, there are three personal resources, capitals or 'ways of knowing' that we need to invest in to make sure that we are in a position to pick and choose the jobs that we want to do and the roles and organisations that we want to work in.

Knowing How: This is the idea of 'human capital' and covers everything needed to do a job well – the skills, experience, knowledge and attributes that you must have to excel in the particular role you are doing or hoping to do next.

Knowing Why: This encompasses motivation, identity and clear career goals. People who 'know why' have a good level of self-awareness and a clear idea of who they want to be, where they want to end up and why this matters to them.

Knowing Whom: This is your social capital – the people in your life who can help you. The help can come in different forms. It could be broad social support – people who can cheer you up, boost your self-esteem or listen when

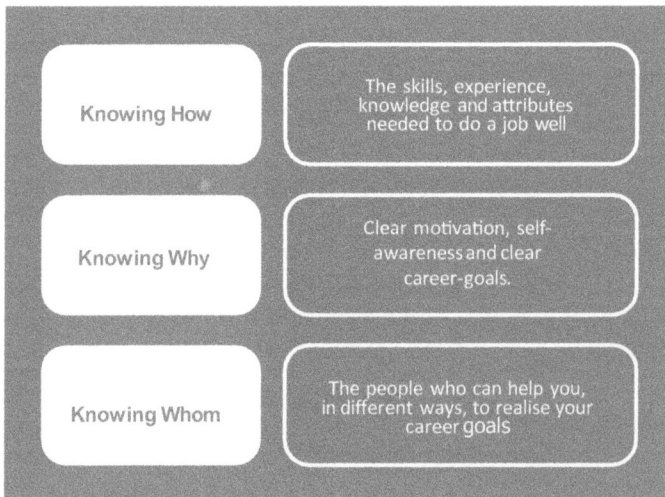

Figure 12.1 Arthur and Fillippi's Intelligent Career Framework.

you need to talk. Or it could be more tangible support, with people who could mentor and guide you, offer insights into a particular role or industry or perhaps even alert you to specific opportunities.

All three ways of knowing boost your chances of getting a job and excelling while you are there, and the three knowings also interact with each other. For example, a clear sense of knowing why will help you to identify the skills that you need (knowing how), or give you the motivation you need to attend a networking event (knowing whom).

Critical viewpoint

The Intelligent Career Framework (ICF) is an offshoot of Michael Arthur's idea of the Boundaryless Career, which aims to describe modern career paths. The assumption behind it is that in the old days, career paths were highly boundaried – we would choose a career, a location and an organisation, and stick with them, progressing steadily up a rigid and predetermined career ladder. These days, according to Arthur, there are no such boundaries. Our career paths are far less linear and predestined, and we are likely to make all sorts of moves and shifts, twists and turns throughout our working lives.

The truth of it is that both of these positions are somewhat overstated. The evidence is clear that there really hasn't been very much of a change in job tenure (how long people stay in a job) over the last five decades: a job for life was never universal, and it is still, now, a reality for many.

But while these central ideas are perhaps inflated, there is no doubt that the world of work is changing rapidly, and we would all do well to think about taking control of our own employability and career development, to make sure that, whatever happens, we continue to be relevant. Whether or not you buy into the narrative that the job for life is dead, these three resources will help you to have choices about what you do and how you do it throughout your career.

The ICF in practice

1) *Individual self-audit:* The ICF can be used as a tool to boost self-awareness. You could share the model explicitly with your clients and invite them to rate themselves on each of the three knowings, giving themselves perhaps a score out of 10 on how confident or well equipped they feel about each. They will then be able to identify where their strengths and weaknesses are, and you can discuss, together, techniques for building their resources.

2) *To structure career education:* The framework could be used as the structure of a workshop or career education programme. Start the session or programme by sharing the framework with your clients and then offer some specific exercises for each of the three knowings.

3) *Specific exercises:*

Knowing How. A job description is often the best place to start with this. You could use the job description of a specific job your client wants to apply for, a more aspirational one within a field they are considering or perhaps a common path for alumni from their particular course or school. Ask your client(s) to look through the job description and person specification, item by item, and give themselves a score – (perhaps 1, no skills; 2, some skills; 3, good skills) for each. You can then identify the areas that need some work and discuss approaches for boosting their skills.

Knowing Why: Helping clients to work out what 'career success' means to them could be a good place to start (see the suggestions in Chapter 10), perhaps inviting them to identify someone they know who has had a fulfilling career, or thinking about their own retirement party and imagining what they would like their boss to say in a speech. A possible selves exercise can also work very well to help clients identify their specific career goals – ask your client to imagine themselves in five years' time, living a positive and fulfilling life. Gradually, step by step ask them to describe each part of their lives – their home, their relationships, their leisure time and then their job. This focus on their future identity, rather than just their future work, can be a useful way to get to what matters for them. I describe this in the Practice tips box on page 76.

Knowing Whom: You could ask your clients to map their networks – perhaps drawing concentric circles on a piece of paper with themselves in the middle, their family in the next ring, close friends next and their larger circle of acquaintances in the outer ring. You could ask them to think about what support each of these people could give them in terms of their career search. Then ask them to think about any gaps – perhaps give them a few prompts for this. For example, who can support them emotionally during their job search? Who could help them refine their CV? Do they know anyone who is working in the field they are interested in? You could also talk about LinkedIn here. I am personally a bit ambivalent about LinkedIn – research seems to show that spending too long on it does terrible things for your confidence – but it is a useful networking tool, and your clients might benefit from a good LinkedIn profile and some prompters for how to use it to reach out and connect with relevant professional contacts.

Key takeaways

The Intelligent Career Framework suggests that there are three ways of 'knowing' that can help us build up our bank of employability resources:

- Knowing How refers to the knowledge, skills and attributes needed to do a job well.

- Knowing Why focuses on our motivation for work and the clarity of our career goals.

- Knowing Whom is our social network – the people we know who can help us meet our career goals.

The ICF can be used as a framework to help clients audit their own employability skills and offers some specific exercises to help clients build or invest in their resources.

Psychological Capital

Introduction

The idea of Psychological Capital (PsyCap) was developed in the 1980s by Fred Luthans. Luthans was an organisational psychologist and was trying to identify the personal resources that enabled employees to thrive within the workplace. As career professionals, we want to equip clients to flourish when they actually start work, so this in itself is relevant to us. But in addition, these qualities have more recently been shown to help people actually get jobs – which we know is often the more immediate concern.

The PsyCap model uses the metaphor of 'capital' – drawing on the work of the sociologist Bourdieu, who used this term as a way to describe any kind of resource that can help you to get ahead. Luthans defines 'psychological capital' as the mental resources that foster workplace wellbeing.

HERO

There are four specific psychological resources identified. They go by the acronym 'HERO': **H**ope, **E**fficacy (elsewhere it's known as self-efficacy, but here it's just efficacy to allow the *HERO* acronym to work), **R**esilience and **O**ptimism. Psychological Capital is described as a *higher-order construct* which relates to the synergy of the four resources. Each of the resources, individually, has a positive impact on wellbeing and can boost your chances of identifying, getting and excelling in your chosen job. But put them together and they have even more power – nourishing each other and providing a psychological boost that is more than the sum of the four individual parts.

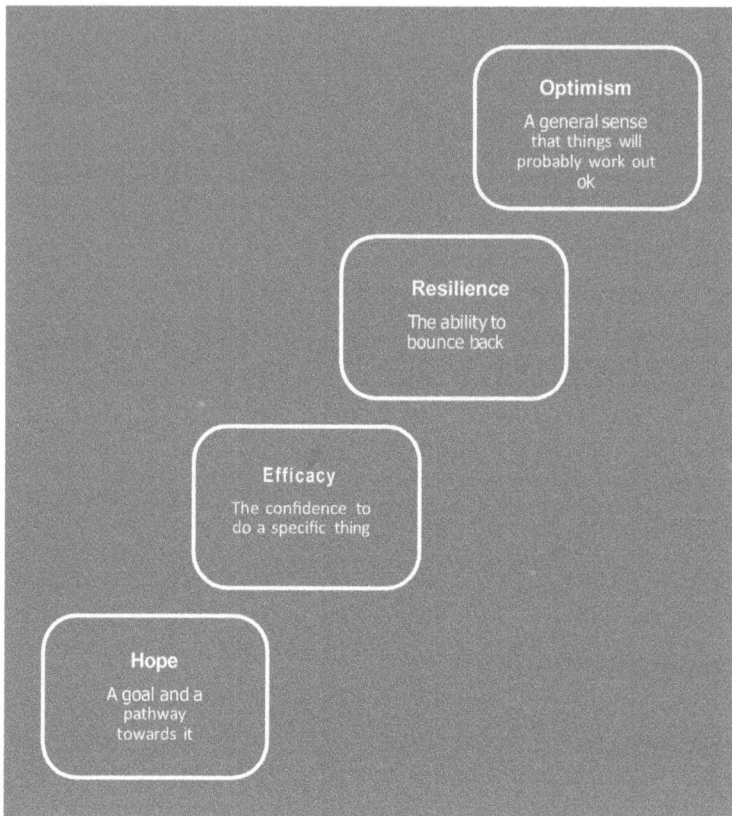

Figure 12.2 Luthans' Theory of Psychological Capital.

Hope: This is one of those terms that has a very specific meaning within psychological research. In general conversation, the word hope refers to a desire about the future, often referring to things outside our control – *I hope it's not going to rain, I hope I win the lottery this weekend.* But in this context, hope is very particularly defined: having a specific goal, and a clear pathway to that goal. In career terms then, hope might be knowing that you really want to become a nurse, and having a good understanding that you will be able to get there by doing well in your exams and applying to university or an apprenticeship programme to study nursing.

Efficacy: We have come across efficacy (self-efficacy) elsewhere in the book, so do have another look at the ideas in Chapter 7 if you want to remind yourself about it. But broadly, efficacy is a measure of context-specific confidence – so to continue the example above, if you want to become a nurse, your efficacy would be a sense of confidence that you will be able to get good grades in your exams, you will be able to secure a place where you can study nursing and there will be a job for you at the end of it.

Resilience: This is another characteristic that has been seen in the careers literature in recent years, as people have become very aware of how valuable it is. I've heard resilience described as your *bounce-back-ability* – the ease with which you cope with setbacks, learn from them and get right back on course. Resilience has been shown in the empirical literature to be linked with all sorts of positive outcomes. Resilient people find difficult situations less stressful, they are more creative about finding solutions and they stick at things longer – all great qualities to help with a job hunt.

Optimism: Optimism is about having a generally positive outlook and having a sense that, on balance, things are likely to work out okay. Optimistic people are not unrealistic; in fact the literature describes it explicitly as *'having a staunch view of reality'*, which reflects a clear understanding of some of the gritty realities of life. But optimists nevertheless assume that things will probably go well. This optimism leads to people setting stretch goals, trying hard and finding creative solutions to problems; they do all this because their optimism makes them believe that it's worth putting in the effort, as it will probably pay off.

PsyCap in practice

Hope

The focus of this exercise is on identifying multiple pathways towards your goals.

Step 1:

First, ask your clients to think about one specific goal. The goal needs to be specific and clear. Then encourage your client to identify as many different pathways or routes to achieving that goal as they can. These can be realistic, ambitious, fanciful or impossible – the goal in this part of the exercise is just to get creative and think of as many as possible. If you are working with groups, at this point, invite your clients to share their goals with a few peers or a partner, and then each member of the group can help with the brainstorming, identifying a number of alternative routes to success. Simply seeing that there are multiple routes can help your clients feel more hopeful about their chances of success.

Step 2:

Ask your client to identify three or four of the most promising pathways. These could be promising because they are easy to do or because they have a high chance of success. Get your client to develop an action plan for each of these pathways, identifying what they would need to do, the steps involved, the barriers they may face and the support they would need. Again, if you are working with groups, this could be a good activity to do collaboratively.

Step 3:

Finally, ask your client to pick one path to start with and commit to the first step. They can then keep the other pathways in reserve just in case, or until they are needed.

Efficacy We have covered practical approaches to efficacy elsewhere in the book – have a look at Chapter 7 for some ideas.

Resilience

Step 1:

Ask your client to identify a recent setback (work, school or personal). Ask them to write down all of the immediate reactions they had to this setback – emotions, thoughts and behaviours.

Step 2:

In Step 2 ask them to reflect on the experience. Specifically, you could ask:

- What was the impact of the setback?
- What aspects were in their control?
- What aspects were beyond their control?
- What did they do about the aspects they could control?
- What else could they have done?

Reminding them of a time when they coped successfully with a setback can help them feel more confident about their ability to cope in the future and less concerned that a single setback will mean the end of the line.

Optimism

Doors closed / doors open

Ask your client to think about a time in their life when a door closed – when something went wrong, and they missed out on an opportunity. Then invite them to think about what happened afterwards and what events or opportunities they experienced that only happened because of the missed opportunity – the doors that opened. Encourage them to reflect on the experience and to think about how that happened and what helped them to identify and capitalise on the opportunity.

DOORS CLOSED / DOORS OPEN EXERCISE WITH AN UNDERGRADUATE

Liz Richardson

I was working with a final-year student who had been rejected from a whole load of quite prestigious graduate training schemes and was feeling quite despondent about his future. He was thinking that he might just need to draw a line under this particular kind of career plan but just couldn't imagine anything else leading to any kind of good future. I think he had just been so focused on these graduate training schemes and had sort of hitched himself to that wagon in terms of his whole identity and his whole vision of his future life, so of course, he was struggling to make his peace with a different kind of future. And he also just felt like a bit of a failure. I was trying to encourage him to think about different alternative paths and to be very positive about these, but I didn't feel I was breaking through.

I was thinking about what I could do to just help him to feel a bit more optimistic about his own future, and I thought about the *doors closed / doors open* exercise. I asked him whether he could think of a time in the past when a door had been closed to him – when he hadn't managed to do the thing he wanted. He talked about when he was rejected by Oxford University when he was in sixth form. That had clearly been quite a blow for him, and he had found it a difficult thing to make peace with. But then I asked him how things had worked out and whether he could think about any doors that had opened for him – were there any good things that had happened to him as a consequence of that rejection? That really seemed to light something up inside him. He talked about how much of a good time he'd had at university, his group of friends and then his face really lit up when he thought about his girlfriend – he was clearly very committed to her, and he'd met her on his course and wouldn't have met her at Oxford. That just seemed to help him recognise that not going to Oxford, although still clearly painful for him, had actually led to three fabulous years. I think that this helped open the door to the idea that there might be other options for his future career that, even though they might not be quite as appealing, might still lead to something good.

139

Key takeaways

PsyCap consists of four distinct psychological resources that can boost an individual's chances of getting and succeeding in their chosen occupation:

- *Hope* – having a clear goal and identifying a path leading towards it;

- *Efficacy* – context-specific confidence;

- *Resilience* – the ability to bounce back after a setback;

- *Optimism* – an assumption that things will probably work out.

PsyCap is a higher-order construct, which means that while each of the resources is useful on its own, there is a real synergy when the four are combined.

Psycho-Social Model of Employability

Introduction

I struggled a bit to decide on the final model within this chapter. My problem was both that there were so many to choose from, and that they all basically included the same characteristics. I've picked this one, from 2004 by Fugate (pronounced Few-gate), Kinicki and Ashforth, partly because I don't think it's very well known but also because I like the way the authors conceptualise and write about the constructs. This model is also of interest because it is more focused on mid-career transitions rather than initial career choice, so it is perhaps particularly relevant to those of you working with career changers or with clients facing redundancy or other kinds of job loss.

The Psycho-Social Model of Employability

The authors define employability as being able to identify and realise career opportunities, and their version of it lies at the intersection of three dimensions: career identity, personal adaptability and social and human capital. The model focuses on the combination of environmental and individual factors, which we have seen elsewhere, but one thing I think this model particularly emphasises is the relationships between the different dimensions: employability, according to this model, isn't based on three separate dimensions, but on a combination of all three. As with the ICF that we covered earlier in the chapter, the psycho-social model has been developed with the modern working world in mind – highlighting the importance of employability as an ongoing, lifelong endeavour – and the authors highlight the influence of change, both within the workplace and within ourselves. They note the shift in who is responsible for career management, which was once the organisation, but is now the individual worker, and they propose

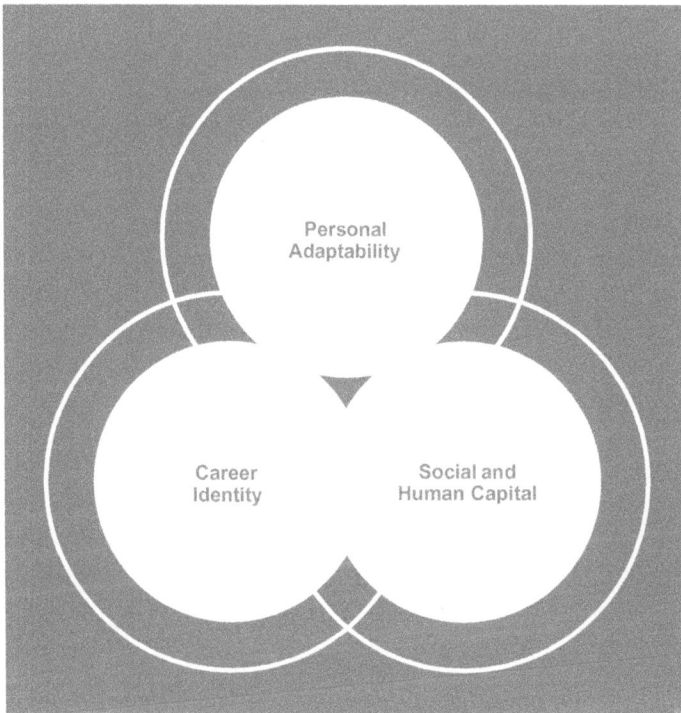

Figure 12.3 Fugate, Ashforth and Kinicki's Psycho-Social Model of Employability.

that these three constructs can help people to become more adaptable and therefore be more in control of their own careers.

At the heart of the model is the idea of *person-centred active adaptation*, which is about people making their own choices about their values and aims, and being proactive about changing themselves or their environment to achieve their goals.

Personal Adaptability: Adaptable people are those who are willing and able to change particular aspects of themselves to meet the needs of the context, gaining the experience and developing the skills that are needed. Fugate and colleagues note that optimism (feeling positive about a likely outcome), self-efficacy (domain-specific self-belief) and an internal locus of control (believing that you have control over what happens to you) all enhance a person's ability or inclination to adapt.

Career Identity: Career identity is about '*Who I am*' and '*Who I want to be*'. The authors describe it here as a longitudinal concept which I think is quite an interesting idea, and one that really makes sense, encompassing past, present and future. Aligning with the idea of narrative – or a storytelling approach – the authors emphasise that it is not so much what you've done that matters, but more the meaning you make from these experiences. This allows for a comparison between past, present and future selves as individuals compare *who they were* with *who they are* and *who they want to be.* The comparison between past and present can allow them to see how far they have come, and the comparison between present and future allows people to work out what they need to do, or how they need to change or adapt, to achieve their goals.

Social and Human Capital: We've come across these before. Social capital is your network of potentially helpful people, and human capital is a measure of your ability to actually do the job in question. Fugate and colleagues describe social capital here as being the goodwill inherent in your social networks. I like that way of looking at it, seeing it not just as the people you know, but more as a measure of the way those people feel towards you and the lengths they are willing and able to go to help.

The reciprocal relationships between the three dimensions are an important part of this model. If you've got a clear career identity, you are likely to be more motivated to adapt, and that will boost your human capital. Strong social capital will help you to know what kind of human capital you need, which will then help to ensure that the ways in which you adapt will be useful for your career identity.

The authors suggest a number of benefits this kind of employability can bring.

- First, it can be useful for people facing redundancy or job loss: high levels of employability can help people see job loss as less damaging and feel more optimistic about identifying alternative opportunities.
- Secondly, employability can help people to cope, as it encourages openness to change and a strong social network, and it can boost what they describe as 'coping efficacy' – your confidence in your ability to cope.
- Finally, it can help with the job hunt itself – it brings clearer goals and more motivation, so is likely to lead to more effort, more persistence and a more satisfactory outcome in the end.

The Psycho-Social model in practice

Personal adaptability

Boosting adaptability is all about encouraging people to see alternatives. It's very easy to become trapped in rigid thinking – sometimes because it's comfortable to carry on doing things the way you've always done them, and it can be scary to push yourself to try something new. This fear can limit your thinking, sometimes to the point that you genuinely can't see any alternatives. A useful way to trick your mind is to imagine that you are someone else. Ask your client to think about a challenge they are currently facing. Then ask them to identify a couple of different people – perhaps someone they admire and someone who is very different from them. Get them to think about how those two people would respond to their current dilemma. What would they think? How would they feel and what would they do? Then ask your client to reflect on the differences – is there any way in which they might want to adapt their behaviour in light of the exercise?

Career identity

A career timeline allows people to reflect on their past experiences and identify possible pathways forward. Invite your client to take a piece of paper and draw a timeline of their career so far – this tends to work better with clients who have left education and spent some time in the workplace but can be adapted to any group. Ask them to identify specific pivotal moments or turning points, and perhaps to think about times when they were particularly satisfied. This can be a great tool for reflecting on the past. Then ask them to map the next ten years out and invite them to think about any key events and what kinds of things will make them happy.

Human and social capital

I've talked about some relevant exercises to boost human and social capital in previous chapters. If your client knows the area they want to go for, a job description can help them analyse their job-specific human capital – ask them to go through the person specification and consider how well they can evidence each point. Then you can work together to create an action plan to enhance their human capital where they need it.

If your client isn't quite ready to identify a job idea, you could use something like a strengths exercise to help them think more broadly about what they can contribute to the workplace. Use some strengths cards or an online assessment, and then talk about their key strengths – perhaps thinking about roles where their key strengths could be particularly useful.

Key takeaways

The psycho-social model defines employability is the ability to identify and realise career opportunities.

It conceptualises employability as a combination of:

- Personal adaptability;
- Career identity;
- Human and social capital.

Each is important on its own, but together they really make an impact on your ability to get the job you want.

Chapter 13
Theories for career transitions

Overview

Career transitions, whether they are positive or negative, planned or unexpected, are common and are almost always stressful. Transition theories can help us understand how our clients might be feeling and how we can help them cope with or capitalise on the changes. In this chapter, we will be looking at three theories:

- *Transition Theory;*
- *Career Shocks;*
- *Post-Job-Loss Career Growth.*

Introduction

Career transitions are extremely common these days, and working with clients who are anticipating or going through a career shift of some sort is a core part of the work of many career professionals. I don't entirely buy into the narrative about the death of a job for life (I talked about this in more detail in Chapter 12), but I think we can probably all agree that career paths these days are rarely stable, predictable and linear. With longer lifespans, rising retirement ages, the cost of living crisis and the increasing fast pace of change in the workplace, people are working for many decades and are likely to face a number of voluntary or enforced changes along the way.

We know that the nature of career transitions can vary widely – from minor shifts to wholesale transformations. They can be positive or negative, often both at the same time; they can be within the control of the individual or a result of external pressures; they can be anticipated or surprising, and they can be generated by work-related changes, personal developments or even world events.

As career professionals, we are probably more likely to come across negative and unexpected transitions in our work – clients who have lost their jobs or who have dropped out of their courses. Sometimes our role will be about rebuilding self-esteem and boosting resilience as we help them pick themselves up, dust themselves off and start all over again. But sometimes a job loss requires a whole new career plan as the individual may have to re-think their entire future. If your hopes and dreams for the future are shattered, and part of your identity stripped away, it can be very hard to adjust, and trying to rebuild your life from this point can take considerable effort.

Of course, not all transitions are bad, even those that might look worrying at the time, and not all transitions turn into crises. But it's probably fair to say that almost all transitions come with a degree of stress, and anything we can do to help our clients cope with this can be a useful addition to our professional toolkit, helping clients make sense of the transition, minimise stress, capitalise on opportunities and adapt smoothly to their new identity.

In this chapter, we will look at three theories that can help to make sense of career transitions. First, we will look at Schlossberg's transition theory, which explains how people adapt to transitions. We then turn to Akkerman's idea of Career Shocks, which focuses on the career-related impact of external events beyond the control of the individual. Finally, we look at Waters and Strauss' optimistic theory of post-job-loss career growth, which highlights the conditions needed to help clients capitalise on a job loss to boost their career development.

Schlossberg's transition theory

Introduction
People's responses to any kind of transition will vary tremendously – different people can react quite differently to the same kind of event, and one individual can even respond very differently to the same kind of transition at different stages in their lives. One key bit of learning for all career professionals is that we should never make assumptions about how an individual might be feeling about a transition – the most seemingly positive news can lead to distress, and an apparently negative event can offer someone great relief.

Schlossberg's theory was developed as a framework for counsellors to help them analyse and evaluate the transitions of their clients and then to develop possible interventions to help them. It focuses on people's ability to cope with transitions and offers an explanation for how and why people react the way that they do. The model helps us support individuals towards *positive adaptation*, which is the point at which an individual has stopped being preoccupied by the transition and has accepted their new status as part of their lives. The model was developed as a more general approach to counselling but has been widely used in writing about career transitions.

Transition Theory

The model has three stages:

1. Approaching transitions: Transition identification;
2. Taking stock of coping resources: The 4S System;
3. Taking charge: Strengthening resources.

1. *Approaching transitions.* In this first stage, we identify the nature of the transition and consider what our clients might need. Transition identification is about the client telling their story, and our job here is to help them articulate the nature of the transition as it appears to them. In order to have a good idea of what the transition means to the individual, it can be useful to think about three things here: the type of transition, the context of the transition, and the impact of the transition.

- *Type of transition.* Transitions can be anticipated or unexpected. Anticipated transitions are usually easier to adjust to, although our reactions to them can still come as a surprise to us. They can be event

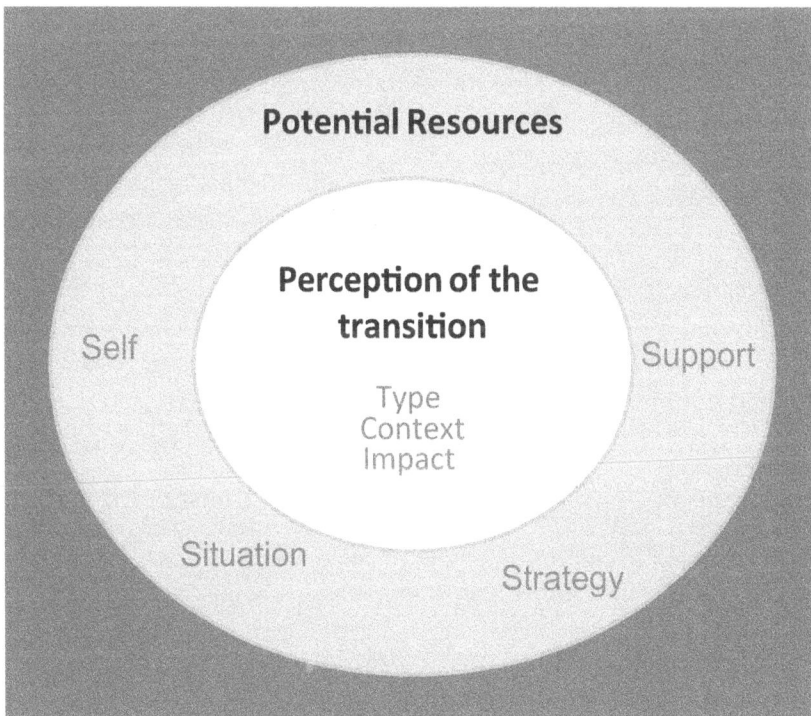

Figure 13.1 Schlossberg's transition theory.

transitions (something happening such as an organisational merger or a new job) or non-event transitions (something that you expected not happening such as not getting a promotion or not getting pregnant).

- *Context for the transition.* The context is both personal and societal. The context for the individual could be related to their life stage, their career goals, their finances or their family set-up. The societal context could relate to social norms, to the local labour market or to global events.
- *The impact of the transition.* The consequences of a transition can be surprising, individual and long lasting. A job loss could have a series of practical implications but also may have an impact on the person's sense of identity, self-worth and confidence. It will also have an impact on their daily life, routines and social support.

2. *Taking stock of coping resources*: The four Ss framework helps to explain how the individual perceives the transition and how well equipped they are to cope with it. It highlights four important characteristics of any transition (situation, self, support and strategies) and offers some questions that we can ask our clients to help them understand the meaning they have made from their own transitions.

Situation

- *The role change*: Have they gained a role (e.g. a promotion) or lost a role (e.g. retirement)?
- *The emotions*: Do they feel positive or negative, or (perhaps most common) a bit of both?
- *The timing*: Is it the right time for them to be making a change? This could be related to their life stage (losing your job when your partner is on parental leave is more challenging than at a time when you are both working full time), society (facing a job hunt in your late 50s is harder than in your mid-30s) or their career (sometimes the option of redundancy can come just when you are ready to make a change).
- *Expectations:* Whether they had been anticipating the change, or whether it came as a shock – bearing in mind that sometimes our response to an event can surprise us, even if the event itself is expected.

Self

People's different responses to an event are based on a number of factors.

- *Demographic characteristics:* Age or life stage, gender, ethnicity and socio-economic status can have an impact on how easily an individual can adapt to their new status.
- *Personality characteristics* such as an individual's degree of optimism, confidence, their degree of agency, values and their sense of identity will help some people adapt more quickly than others.

Support

This is all about the environment in which the individual is facing the change, and the support they can access or choose to access.

- *Interpersonal support systems*: Including intimate relationships (most often a partner), the family unit (parents or children depending on the individual) and a network of friends. These sources of interpersonal support cushion the blow, boost a sense of ongoing stable identity and offer practical support.
- *Institutional support*: This can come from the organisation that caused the job loss, in the form of any financial settlement or practical support available, or from other institutions such as religious communities or social welfare. Career support can fall into this category too.

Strategies

Different coping strategies can be aimed at different kinds of outcomes.

- *Responses that modify the situation*: These can actually reduce the problem itself, for example, negotiating with the line manager.
- *Responses that control the meaning of the problem*: These are psychological strategies that can help clients reframe the problem. For example, they could think about the positives of their situation, focus on the bits of their current or previous job that they didn't really like or consider what they could do with the additional time they now have on their hands.
- *Responses that help to manage stress*: Talking to friends or practising mindfulness.

3. *Taking charge: Strengthening resources.* The final stage is when you help your client think about how they can capitalise on the resources they already have and how they can build or develop those that they might be lacking.

Schlossberg's Transition model in practice

Narrative approaches: This isn't the first time I have mentioned narrative approaches in this book (and do go back to the case study with Dr Helen Cooper in Chapter 6 to see how she uses narratives in her career practice). Here they are useful because they can allow you and your client to understand the transition from their perspective, helping to ensure that you don't make any assumptions about what is good, bad or difficult about your client's situation.

Practical support: We note throughout this chapter that financial and social support can really make a difference in someone's ability to cope well with a transition. As a career professional, you can help your client think about their finances, perhaps offering them an opportunity to role-play a negotiation conversation with their organisation, or making sure they know about any welfare benefits they might be entitled to. You might also be in a position to foster opportunities for your clients to meet each other. If you are working with more than one person who finds themselves in a similar situation, you could set up some group workshops and encourage peer mentoring.

Solution-focused coaching: This is an approach to career support that can help people reframe their current situation and explore their existing personal resources. One technique for identifying personal resources is to ask your client to talk about a time in their past when they had to cope with a difficult situation. Ask them to tell you about that time and what they did to manage the situation. Then ask them, quite specifically, to start identifying the strengths or characteristics within them that enabled them to get through that difficult time. I would use a phrase like '*What was it about you that enabled you to cope?*' and then help them really drill down to identify their strengths. You can then, together, think about how they could use those characteristics to help them in their current situation.

🔑 Key takeaways

People will respond to different transitions in different ways, so it's always important to ask your clients to tell the story of their transition in their own way.

It can be useful to think about the type of transition, the context of the transition and the impact of the transition.

People will have different resources that can help them to cope. The four Ss model categorises these potential resources in terms of:

- Situation;
- Self;
- Support;
- Strategies.

It can be useful to discuss these with clients to help them identify and build on their ability to cope.

Career Shocks

Introduction

There is a message running across this whole book that career development is a product of both individual and environmental factors. Some theories focus very much on one or the other of these (e.g. Law's Community Interaction highlights environmental factors, and Arthur's Intelligent Career Framework focuses on individual agency). Other theories, such as Patton and McMahon's Systems Theory Framework, try to integrate both types of factors. Career Shocks is one such theory that understands that career development is very much a product of a combination of the individual and the environment, and it focuses on individuals' responses to environmental events. Akkermans felt that the recent career development literature had been less focused on external, uncontrollable factors in recent decades and proposed the idea of Career Shocks as a way to redress this balance. He argues that in the current climate, where we are just beginning to understand the profound impact that AI may have on work, organisations and careers, we should be more interested than ever in the impact of unexpected, uncontrollable external events, suggesting that it is really important to try to understand how people can best survive and thrive in the face of unexpected events.

A Career Shock happens when an unexpected external event makes you start to question your own career. It is defined as a disruptive and extraordinary event caused by factors outside your control. Other theories cover the impact of unexpected events on career paths (e.g. Planned Happenstance that we cover in Chapter 8, and the Chaos Theory of Careers that we don't have space for in this book but which you might want to look up), but Akkerman's idea of Career Shocks is different in that it encompasses events that aren't necessarily directly work-related but which change the way you think about your work.

Career Shocks can come from all angles – they can be personal or interpersonal, within the organisation or outside it. Examples include the death of a parent, getting a promotion, not getting a promotion, relocating because of a spouse's job, having children, illness, an economic crash, being made redundant, an earthquake or unexpected exam results. And in general, the bigger the event, the more destabilising properties it will have.

> ### The Career Shock of Covid-19
>
> The recent pandemic was an interesting example of a Career Shock that impacted many of us. This was a global health event that, for most of us, wasn't directly work-related, but nevertheless led many of us to re-think how we worked, where we worked and why we worked.
>
> For some, it was all about the potential for working from home that we tried out during the lockdowns. We realised that we could, for the most part, work quite effectively without going into the office, and saw how much time, money and stress we could eliminate from our lives by basing ourselves at home. This led many people to move away from the cities and towns, keeping up with colleagues online and perhaps going to work just one or two days each week.
>
> For others, it was the thinking that we were able to do with so much extra time on our hands. During the lockdowns, we had to stop much of our socialising and leisure activities, and this offered some of us a lot of time to think. We had the opportunity to reflect on our lives, and for some this led to the decision to make some different work choices.
>
> A final group started to reconsider their values and priorities. Many people were directly touched by loved ones who were ill or even lost their lives to Covid, and these experiences caused some to question their purpose in life or their role in society. As a result, some decided to change their career direction, perhaps to look for work that better aligned with their values. Despite the horrendous conditions that we all witnessed in hospitals, there was a huge surge in the number of people applying to nursing and medicine in the years immediately after the pandemic, which seems to have been an example of this.

An individual's reaction to the shock will be influenced by their pre-existing feelings about their work. People who were satisfied at work before the shock are more likely to take their time to engage in steady, rational, conscious critical reflection about their careers and next steps. Those who were dissatisfied pre-shock are more likely to fling themselves spontaneously into action after the shock – perhaps not pausing for long to weigh the pros and cons or think about the consequences. For people who felt neutral about their jobs, a Career Shock can make them realise that they weren't happy – as the literature says, the shock can surface *latent disquiet*.

The characteristics of Career Shocks

There are four core characteristics of Career Shocks:

Deliberation: A Career Shock is something that makes you think, reflect on or question your career. Not all life shocks will be Career Shocks – the death of a loved one can affect you profoundly, but it may not lead you to question your career. Alternatively, it may cause you to question your values and what you want from life, and this may lead you to start wondering what life would be like if you worked in a different sector.

Controllability: A Career Shock is to some degree beyond the control of the individual, although the degree of controllability may vary from one shock to another. Redundancy is an example of a Career Shock that is probably entirely beyond your control, whereas getting a new job will be to some degree your choice (whether you apply, how much effort you put into interview preparation), although the final decision about whether you get the job or not is down to the hiring organisation. In other circumstances, the event itself can be within your control while the impact of the event isn't. Having a baby, for example, for many, is a controllable event, but the impact of the event on someone's career may be completely out of their hands.

Predictability: A lot of the literature on external events assumes that the events are always unpredictable, but Career Shocks can vary in the degree to which they are expected or unexpected. With redundancy, for example, the individual may be given a considerable amount of notice, or they may learn about the decision on the very day they need to leave.

Emotional response: Career Shocks can be both positive and negative and can lead to both positive and negative changes. Most research suggests that how you feel about the shock itself is related to the nature of the career outcomes, so positive Career Shocks lead to positive career outcomes and negative shocks to negative outcomes. But this is not always the case, and some studies show that negative shocks can lead to positive career outcomes, in particular for those who weren't all that happy in their jobs in the first place but who needed an external push to action.

How we react to the Career Shock has a clear impact on our career development and our chances of career success. Whether the event is a positive or negative one, we can choose to respond either actively or passively.

A promotion, for example, would generally be considered a good event, and 9 times out of 10 would make someone feel positive. But people can respond in different ways to a promotion. Some might be inspired to work harder, perhaps because they want to demonstrate that they deserve the new position, or perhaps because they are excited to have an interesting new challenge ahead. This is a proactive response and is likely to lead to positive career growth. Others might feel that the promotion marks the end of their striving – they might feel that they have now got to where they want to be, they have proved to the world that they are worthy of a senior role, and can now can relax into their new corner office and enjoy spending their new salary. This is a more passive approach and might lead to career stagnation.

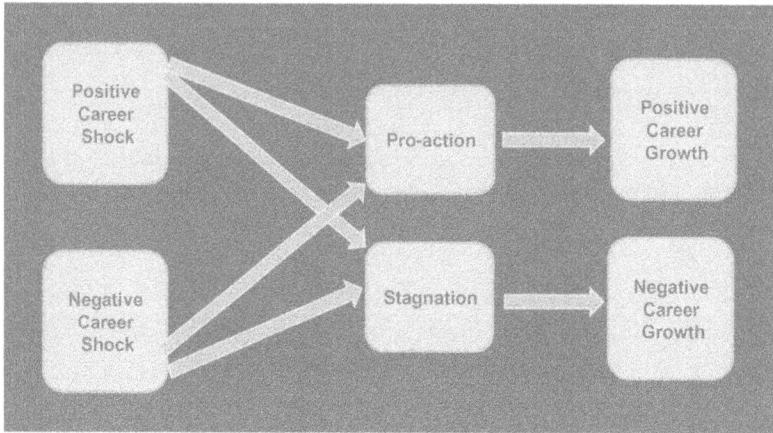

Figure 13.2 Akkerman's Career Shocks.

The death of a loved one is an example of a negative shock. It might lead someone to reassess their life values, as they confront how short life is. A proactive response might be to change career direction and find something that feels more meaningful. A more passive response might be to become disheartened with the meaninglessness of corporate life and start to disengage at work.

Mitigating factors

There are two key factors that have been shown to lead to a more proactive response to a Career Shock. First, a sense of agency. People who feel that they have some ownership of their lives and careers, and who believe that their actions will have an impact on their future, are more likely to respond in a proactive way to a Career Shock. Have a look at some of the ideas in Chapter 8 for theories and practical ideas for boosting agency in clients. The second is social support. Support from family and friends has been shown to increase the chances of a proactive response and positive career growth following a Career Shock.

Career Shocks in practice

- *Writing:* A Career Shock often triggers reflections about personal or professional values, and writing sessions can be a great way to help people identify and articulate what matters to them. There is something about the process of translating ideas into words that helps people clarify their thinking (this is of course the basis of much of our guidance or coaching work) and putting the words down on paper can help take their thinking to a deeper level. This kind of exercise also gives clients something tangible to take away, re-read and reflect on after the session, which can be particularly useful. They can also then choose which bits of their written piece to share with you and which bits to keep to themselves. This potential opportunity for total confidentiality can free people up to be more authentic.

One writing technique involves asking your client, at the start of a session, to spend five minutes putting their thoughts down on paper – just writing a stream of consciousness, getting all of the thoughts swirling round in their minds on to the page, without any particular agenda or prompt questions. When the five minutes is up, ask them to read their writing over to themselves, and invite them to share any reflections with you, or to read out any phrases or passages that they are particularly struck by. This exercise serves to clear their minds and clarify their thoughts which can lead to a more productive and targeted conversation with you.

- *Time to think.* A defining feature of a Career Shock is that it is unexpected. Taking some time to process what has happened, and what it means to your client is therefore particularly helpful. A humanistic approach to active and intent listening can be really powerful, so give them some time and try not to push for a solution or action too soon. One coaching approach from Nancy Kline, called *A Time to Think*, suggests that we should simply ask our clients, '*What do you want to talk about and what would you like to say?*' We then listen intently, offering encouraging responses and just a very few follow-up questions to keep them talking. When the client seems to have come to the end of what they have to say, you follow up with '*What more would you like to say?*' or '*What else do you want to talk about and what would you like to say about that?*' I find the specifics of this approach a bit rigid, but it is definitely useful to remember the power involved in non-judgemental active listening.

Key takeaways

Career Shocks are events outside of the control of an individual that make them question their own career development.

Shocks can come from within an organisation, such as a business takeover, a new boss, or a promotion, or from outside, such as an illness, the death of a loved one or a change in governmental policy.

Shocks can be positive or negative. Usually, negative shocks lead to negative career outcomes, and vice versa, but this isn't always the case.

Post-job-loss career growth

Introduction

Alongside the obvious financial benefits, work fulfils a number of crucial functions for subjective wellbeing: it fills our days, gives structure to our weeks, offers us social interaction and gives us a reason to get up in the morning. It is no great surprise to learn, therefore, that job loss does little for our self-worth and life satisfaction and leads to higher stress levels, depression and anxiety, and lowered self-esteem. Job loss has a significant impact on physical health too, leading to higher levels of drinking, smoking and recreational drug use and actually increasing our risk of death. The effect of job loss and subsequent unemployment can last for years, well into an individual's new career, and it can also have a long-term impact on people's families, affecting even their children's mental health and education. Coupled with these physical and psychological risks are the economic challenges usually associated with job loss and the removal of a social network that can often help people to cope in a crisis.

No wonder that losing a job is acknowledged to be one of the 10 most stressful life events.

But job loss is common. Many of us have worked with clients who have lost their jobs, and perhaps recognise this kind of impact within our clients, and perhaps in our loved ones and ourselves too.

Post-job-loss career growth

The notion of *post-traumatic growth* has garnered a lot of interest in recent decades. This is the process through which people emerge from extremely challenging times in a more positive place, as a direct result of these difficult times: their traumatic experience leads to personal growth. This concept has been applied more recently to the arena of careers, and a number of scholars have explored the idea of '*post-job-loss career growth*', where a redundancy or other forced break can eventually lead to greater job satisfaction and subjective career success than an individual would have experienced had they remained in their previous role. It isn't just about surviving and coping with the job loss, but about rebuilding better – capitalising on new opportunities and creating new identities which they couldn't have done if things had stayed the same.

There are certain conditions that seem to make post-job-loss career growth more likely – some to do with the individual, and others linked to their environment. These are very useful for us to keep in mind. If we know the factors that can help our clients towards a positive future, we can help them create or seek out the most fertile conditions. We can also share the model explicitly with our clients to let them know that a more positive future may be just around the corner.

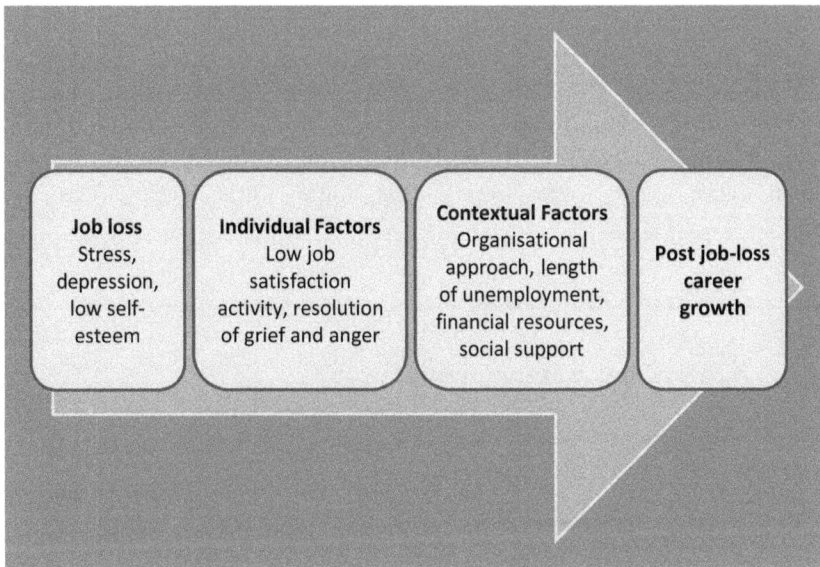

Figure 13.3 The post-job-loss career growth model.

Individual factors

Low job satisfaction: We covered Career Inaction Theory in Chapter 9, which acknowledges the very real role that inertia plays in many career paths. While people who are *really* miserable at work often make the effort to find a new job, people who are *quite* miserable often end up staying put. They might feel that their levels of job satisfaction are good enough, and perhaps they don't want to take on the risks of finding something new. For this group of people – those who are not happy, but not miserable enough to quit – a redundancy can force their hand and give them the motivation to make the change that perhaps they should have made months (or years!) before.

Activity: When your daily routines are gone and the need to set your alarm clock and get up early has been taken away, it can be easy to start to take life at a slower pace. But keeping busy has been shown to help with mental wellbeing, and the more time you can spend on your future career planning and job hunting, the more you are likely to reap rewards.

Resolution of grief and anger: Job loss can have a profound and sometimes lasting impact on your emotions (see box below). This is a completely normal part of the job-loss process, and people will experience and deal with their emotions at different speeds. But while it's completely expected that people will find it emotionally challenging, these negative feelings need to be resolved before someone can fully move on.

Contextual factors

Organisational approach: People find it much easier to make their peace with their situation if they have been treated well by the organisation. An individual needs to understand the rationale for the job loss and see that the process has been conducted fairly. It also helps if they were given a long notice period and if they feel that the organisation has valued them and has tried to support them.

The Kubler-Ross bereavement curve

Elizabeth Kubler-Ross studied the emotions experienced during bereavement. She identified six stages of grief that people typically go through as they accept the loss and eventually adapt to their new life. It has been shown that people experiencing a job loss seem to go through the same six stages, usually (although not inevitably) in the same order:

1. Denial – This can't be happening to me.
2. Anger – I'm absolutely furious that they have done this to me.
3. Bargaining – I'm sure that if I offer to take on some additional responsibilities, they will be happy to keep me.
4. Depression – I'm just really sad about it all.
5. Exploration – I am going to look around to see what else is out there.
6. Acceptance – I have made my peace with the job loss and can start to look forward to my next chapter.

People tend to be at their most emotionally distressed at stage 4, and after that, they become more positive and start to see a brighter future.

There are two particularly useful things that career professionals can do with this information. First, we can share it with our clients to help normalise their feelings and to give them hope. It can be very reassuring to know that the acute emotions you feel following a job loss are completely normal, and to learn that a job loss is often as traumatic to cope with as a bereavement. And it can also be encouraging to know that however you are feeling now, things will probably get better.

Secondly, it can be useful to keep these stages in mind to check that your client hasn't got stuck in an emotional loop. Typically, people move through the stages one by one within a reasonable timeframe, but it's not uncommon for people to get stuck at one of the stages or to find themselves in a doom loop – going back and forth between, say, depression and anger. If you notice this pattern in your client, then it might be a sign that they are in need of some further psychological support, and it might be useful to have a discussion with them about seeing a counsellor to help them make sense of their emotions.

Length of unemployment: During a longer period of unemployment, people can become increasingly disillusioned, and their self-esteem can get steadily worn down. It is definitely useful to encourage clients to focus on finding a new job, but, leaping straight into a new role can also prove problematic, as you don't get a chance to really think about what you want to do next and to make your peace with what has gone before. Try to help your clients find a balance that allows them to take the time they need to make sense of everything that has happened but not to linger too long.

Financial resources: Financial resources can cushion the blow of a job loss and allow people to take the time they need to think things through, process their feelings and make thoughtful, proactive decisions about what to do next. Some organisations can offer a useful redundancy package or perhaps a few months of gardening leave, where you continue to be paid but don't need to work. Alternatively, you may be lucky enough to have a second income at home or be able to move back in with your parents. This kind of financial security means that you can take a bit of time to really think about what you want to do next, and perhaps invest some money in training or even some good career support.

Social support: We should never underestimate the value of a good social network. Having people around you can make such a difference to your sense of self, your self-esteem and your ability to cope with setbacks.

Post-job-loss career growth in practice

Motivational interviewing: After a job loss, clients can feel very negative about the future and start to look at the past through rose-coloured glasses – only remembering the good times. One useful approach to facilitating post-job-loss career growth is to switch this around and encourage your client to focus on the negatives of their previous role and the positives of future possibilities. Motivational interviewing is an approach that can help. One straightforward exercise is to ask your client to rate their satisfaction with their previous job on a scale of 1 – 10. Assuming that they give it a score lower than 10, you can ask them what was not perfect about it and encourage them to articulate, expand on and focus on the negatives. Ask them, *'What was it about the job that wasn't ideal for you?'* Encourage them to dwell on the negatives – *'So you say that your boss wasn't very supportive? Tell me more about that. What sorts of things did they do? How did that make you feel?'* Then encourage them to think about the ways in which things might be better in the future: *'Imagine a future job where you did have a supportive boss. What would that be like? How would you feel about work? What impact would that have on your behaviour?'*

Identity work: Some clients going through a career transition simply want to find another similar job in the same field. For these clients, you will be focusing on job hunting and trying to keep them feeling resilient. Other clients might need to or want to look for a complete change. For these clients, it can be useful to explore different kinds of possible futures. Here is a three-stage intervention that can help clients balance creativity and pragmatism in their career exploration.

i) *Identity play*

Identity play is exploratory rather than goal-focused, and it allows clients to try out a range of new identities to see how they feel about being that new version of themselves. The different identities they explore don't need to be realistic or sensible, this part of the exercise is just about imagining possibilities. Invite your client to think about a wide range of possible versions of themselves – fantasy, aspirational and realistic and just talk about what their lives would be like in the different scenarios.

ii) *Disciplined imagination*

Alongside this identity play, clients should be encouraged to engage in disciplined imagination. This sounds like a contradiction in terms but entails alternating two processes: asking sensible questions (that's the disciplined bit) and generating an unfettered list of possible answers (that's the imagination). The sensible questions could be things like *'What do I like doing?'*, *'What kinds of jobs would value my skills?'*, *'What other people's career paths sound interesting to me?'* and can help the individual develop ideas about realistic possible futures, directions or useful first steps.

iii) *Identity refinement*

The final process is one of refinement. In this, you spend time with your client discussing their ideas and activities, and helping them gradually whittle down the options and make some decisions about the next steps.

POST-JOB-LOSS CAREER GROWTH

Caroline Shepherd

I used this theory with a client who had just lost her job, and I think it really helped her to feel a bit more optimistic. That optimism allowed us to have a richer conversation.

This client, let's call her Paige, was referred to me by a colleague. Paige worked in education and had, just six months before, got what she thought would be her dream job. She had started work as a lecturer at a university, teaching on a counselling degree course. She had completely immersed herself in the new role, loved the students and really enjoyed the job. And then, six months down the line, the university decided to close down the course. Paige was just completely devastated.

I saw Paige a few times, and during our time together, I used two different theories, both of which I think helped. The first was the Kubler-Ross stages of grief. I thought about this when Paige was talking about her feelings, and she said a few things that seemed to resonate with the different stages, talking about not being able to believe that it was happening and then about trying to bargain with the university. I didn't talk to her explicitly about the model, but it helped me to understand her a bit better, and I think it just helped me to be more patient and to wait until she had moved through the stages before trying to get her to start making a plan.

The theory which I did share with her was the post-job-loss career growth theory. Paige was really struggling to see a bright future. She didn't seem able to think creatively or use her imagination to envisage any kind of positive future, and I couldn't manage to get her to consider that there might be a different but positive future out there for her. As a counsellor, she was quite interested in psychological theories, so I thought it might be worth trying to share the theory directly with her, and I believe the fact that it was a theory probably helped to give the ideas some credibility. I explained the concept and suggested that we could just play around with some ideas about her future, just to see whether we might be able to think up any positive solutions. This idea that seemed to unlock something in her, allowing her to think more freely. We talked about all sorts of different ideas without trying to make a decision or a plan of any sort. The next time I saw her, she told me about another new idea that had come to her, which was related to her lovely dogs. She thought about trying to set up her own counselling practice using her dogs (she had two absolutely beautiful and very gentle golden retrievers) as therapy dogs. It was one of those ideas that she almost couldn't believe she hadn't thought about before. It seemed to tick all the boxes. I saw her once more after that, and she came up with what sounded like a good plan of action, which she seemed very committed to and eager to start.

Key takeaways

A job loss will almost always be difficult to cope with and can lead to severe and long-lasting negative emotions.

Sometimes, however, job loss can be a catalyst for positive change, and individuals can end up in a better career position than they would have been had they not lost their job.

People are more likely to end up in a positive place if they didn't love their job but can resolve negative emotions. It also helps if their previous organisation treated them well and if they have some financial and social support.

Final thoughts and next steps

Overview

In this final chapter, I summarise some of the key ideas that have come up time and again in the theories we have covered in the book. I also want to leave you with some ideas about how to make sure that you capitalise on the learning from this book, and to get you thinking about your next CPD project.

Introduction

I think I should start by saying congratulations to you. Congratulations first for being the kind of career professional who wants to engage with theories and who wants to grow, develop and learn more to help your clients. You are a real lifelong learner, and I love that you yourself are modelling the kind of thing we talk to our clients about. That's fantastic. I also want to congratulate you for getting to the end of the book. You might have approached it in a sort of pick-and-mix way – just looking at the ideas to which you are most drawn – or perhaps you've been more systematic, doing each chapter in turn. But either way, I really hope you have found the ideas interesting and the suggestions useful.

Key theoretical ideas

We have looked at a good range of theories in this book. Theories from different countries, developed in different contexts, informed by different academic disciplines and focused on explaining different aspects of career development. So it's interesting that there are some particular ideas or constructs that come up repeatedly.

I thought it might be useful just to bring them all together in this final chapter, as they might be the key ideas that are particularly important to our clients. Even if none of the theories particularly stick with you, I think these three points are useful to keep in mind with every client.

Self-efficacy: This is your confidence to succeed in a particular task – for example, your confidence in your own ability to make a career decision or your confidence to succeed at a job interview. This lies at the heart of Social Cognitive Career Theory, which describes the whole process of making a career choice (Chapter 9). It came up when we looked at the skills needed to navigate careers (Career Adaptability – Chapter 8) and as a way to help clients manage their emotions (Chapter 7). Feeling confident about your ability to succeed makes you set more stretching goals, put a bit more effort into achieving them and boosts your resilience, making you better able to cope when things go wrong.

Broadening experiences: The importance of broadening clients' horizons – exposing them to a wide range of work-related experiences – was highlighted in theories about the process of career development in Chapter 9 (Social Cognitive Career Theory and the Real-World Model of Career Decision-Making), theories about influences in Chapter 6 (Community Interaction and Circumscription and Compromise) and theories to help clients take ownership of their careers in Chapter 8 (Planned Happenstance). Having experience in a range of different workplaces, doing a range of different things, can help in various ways. First it helps with self-awareness: it is through actually doing things that we learn what we are good at and what we enjoy. Then, it helps with option generation – the more occupations we know about, the more we can make informed decisions about our own futures.

Autonomy: Feeling a sense of control over your own career came up in theories to help clients take ownership (Planned Happenstance and Career AdaptAbility in Chapter 8), theories to enhance self-awareness (Self-Determination Theory in Chapter 10) and theories to explain the experiences of marginalised groups (Psychology of Working Theory, Chapter 11). Autonomy is key to helping us feel good about what we are doing. If we feel that we have choices about where we work, what we do and how we do it, then we are likely to feel happier with the decisions we are making and the place we end up.

What next?

Putting your new learning into practice
There are articles published every year that show quite compelling evidence that people often fail to put their new learning into practice. We go on training courses and spend time learning about new ideas and new approaches, and then all too often, we just go back to our old ways. This is very common, but it's such a waste. Happily, there is some empirical evidence that suggests there are two key things that you can do to help you capitalise on your newfound knowledge.

1. *Do it now*

The first thing is to put your learning into practice straight away. You just need to try it out as soon as you can. Don't wait for the perfect moment, don't promise yourself you'll get to it later – just go out and do it straight away. Tomorrow. Today. As soon as you can.

2. *Get other people on board*

Something else that makes a real difference is having supporters. Having a line manager who holds you to account, peers to talk things through with and a supportive environment all really increase your chances of putting your new ideas into practice. Let your team or network know that you've been reading this book – tell them what you've learned and give feedback to them once you've tried something new. I bet they'll find it interesting, and you might even inspire them to do a bit of CPD of their own.

Learning more
You've done an amazing job in getting this far. But don't let it stop here. There is always more to learn. If you still have an appetite for more theories, there are plenty of books and blogs out there that you might find useful. Have a look at the Further Reading section at the end of the book for some ideas.

You may already be a member of a professional body, but if not, this might be useful to explore. The professional bodies usually offer a wide range of different types of CPD, and they are generally of very high quality and reasonably priced. They also offer opportunities to get involved in a community – there are some amazing colleagues working in our field, and sharing ideas with fellow practitioners can be a great way to enhance your own knowledge and make a contribution to the whole profession.

However you decide to take things forward, good luck with it!

Key takeaways

Reading this book is a great start, but you also need to put it into practice.

The sooner you can try some of the ideas out, the better – do it today if you can.

Having a team of people is helpful – talk to your manager and your colleagues.

What's next for you and your CPD?

Further reading

General further reading about theories

Arthur, N., Nealt, R., & McMahon, M. (2019). *Career theories and models at work: Ideas for practice.* CERIC. This is a super book about theories. It goes into a bit more depth than this book, and has lots of good, practical suggestions.

Matthews, R. J. (2017). A theory for everything? Is a knowledge of career development theory necessary to understand career decision making? *European Scientific Journal, 13*(7), 320–334. https://core.ac.uk/download/pdf/236405204.pdf

There are several super blogs and websites written by colleagues in the careers field. Here are three that I refer to a lot, but do trawl the web for others:

Careers in Theory by David Winter: https://careersintheory.wordpress.com/author/careersdwinter/

Running in a Forest by Tom Staunton: https://runninginaforest.wordpress.com/

Career MarcR by Marc Truyens covers a wide range of career theories in a very accessible style: https://marcr.net/marcr-for-career-professionals/career-theory/career-theories-and-theorists/

Further reading
by theory in alphabetical order

Acceptance and Commitment Theory
Hoare, P. N., McIlveen, P., & Hamilton, N. (2012). Acceptance and commitment therapy (ACT) as a career counselling strategy. *International Journal for Educational and Vocational Guidance, 12,* 171–187. https://research.usq.edu.au/download/b560f8c00955fd4f5d59294d5d2568a0da347a3c5f7aee5fffce6f9faf37454f/399648/Hoare_McIlveen_Hamilton_IJEVG_v12n3_AV.pdf

Career AdaptAbilities
Johnston, C. S. (2018). A systematic review of the career adaptability literature and future outlook. *Journal of Career Assessment, 26*(1), 3–30. https://boris.unibe.ch/90741/8/Johnston_Career%20Adaptability%20Review.pdf

Career Construction Theory
Savickas, M. L. (2013). Career construction theory and practice. In S. D. Brown & R. W. Lent (Eds.), Career development and counseling: Putting theory and research to work (2nd ed., pp. 144–180). John Wiley. https://www.hzu.edu.in/uploads/2020/9/Career%20Development%20and%20Counseling_%20Putting%20Theory%20and%20Research%20to%20Work.pdf#page=161

Career Inaction Theory

Verbruggen, M., & De Vos, A. (2020). When people don't realize their career desires: Toward a theory of career inaction. *Academy of Management Review, 45*(2), 376–394. https://repository.uantwerpen.be/docman/irua/6d0104/157796_2020_02_22.pdf

Career Shocks

Akkermans, J., Seibert, S. E., & Mol, S. T. (2018). Tales of the unexpected: Integrating career shocks in the contemporary careers literature. *SA Journal of Industrial Psychology, 44*(1), 1–10.

Wordsworth, R., & Nilakant, V. (2021). Unexpected change: Career transitions following a significant extra-organizational shock. *Journal of Vocational Behavior, 127*, 103555.

Career Success

Heslin, P. A. (2005). Conceptualizing and evaluating career success. *Journal of Organizational Behavior: The International Journal of Industrial, Occupational and Organizational Psychology and Behavior, 26*(2), 113–136. https://www.researchgate.net/profile/Peter-Heslin/publication/227729978_Conceptualizing_and_evaluating_career_success/links/59e1c42eaca2724cbfdfd848/Conceptualizing-and-evaluating-career-success.pdf

Circumscription and Compromise

Gottfredson, L. S. (2005). Using Gottfredson's theory of circumscription and compromise in career guidance and counseling. In *Career development and counseling: Putting theory and research to work* (pp. 71–100). https://www1.udel.edu/educ/gottfredson/reprints/2004theory.pdf

Community Interaction

Bill Law. (1981). *Building on what we know community-interaction.* http://www.law-family.org.uk/hihohiho/memory/cafcit.pdf

Cultural Preparation Process Model

Arulmani, G. (2014). The cultural preparation process model and career development. In G. Arulmani, A. J. Bakshi, F. T. L. Leong, & A. G. Watts (Eds.), *Handbook of career development: International perspectives* (pp. 81–104). Springer International.

Kaleidoscope Career Model

Mainiero, L. A., & Gibson, D. E. (2018). The kaleidoscope career model revisited: How midcareer men and women diverge on authenticity, balance, and challenge. *Journal of Career Development, 45*(4), 361–377.

The Intelligent Career Framework

Arthur, M., Khapova, S., & Richardson, J. (2018). *An intelligent career.* OUP.

PERMA Model

Seligman, M. E. (2011). *Flourish.* Nicholas Brealey Publishing.

Seligman, M. E., & Csikszentmihalyi, M. (2000). *Positive psychology: An introduction* (55,1, p.5). American Psychological Association. https://gacbe.ac.in/pdf/ematerial /18BPS6EL-U3.pdf

Planned Happenstance
Mitchell, K. E., Al Levin, S., & Krumboltz, J. D. (1999). Planned happenstance: Constructing unexpected career opportunities. *Journal of Counseling & Development*, *77*(2), 115–124. https://westallen.typepad.com/files/10.1.1.202.6401.pdf#page=3

Post-job-loss career growth
Waters, L., & Strauss, G. (2016). Posttraumatic growth during unemployment: A qualitative examination of distress and positive transformation. *International Journal of Wellbeing*, *6*(1). https://internationaljournalofwellbeing.org/index.php/ijow/article /view/441

Psycho-Social Model of Employability
Fugate, M., Kinicki, A. J., & Ashforth, B. E. (2004). Employability: A psycho-social construct, its dimensions, and applications. *Journal of Vocational Behavior*, *65*(1), 14–38. https://www.researchgate.net/profile/Blake-Ashforth/publication/222580864 _Employability_A_Psycho-Social_Construct_Its_Dimensions_and_Applications /links/5daf291f92851c577eb99a4a/Employability-A-Psycho-Social-Construct-Its -Dimensions-and-Applications.pdf

Psychological Capital
Carter, J. W., & Youssef-Morgan, C. (2022). Psychological capital development effectiveness of face-to-face, online, and micro-learning interventions. *Education and Information Technologies*, *27*(5), 6553–6575. https://link.springer.com/article/10.1007/ s10639-021-10824-5

The Psychology of Working Theory
Blustein, D. L., Kenna, A. C., Gill, N., & DeVoy, J. E. (2008). The psychology of working: A new framework for counseling practice and public policy. *The Career Development Quarterly*, *56*(4), 294–308.

Real-World Model of Career Decision-Making
https://coachingincareers.blogspot.com/2023/01/career-decisions-in-real-world.html

RIASEC

Nauta, M. M. (2010). The development, evolution, and status of Holland's theory of vocational personalities: Reflections and future directions for counseling psychology. *Journal of Counseling Psychology*, *57*(1), 11. https://www.counseling.org/docs/david -kaplan's-files/nauta.pdf?sfvrsn%3D2

SCCT

Lent, R. W., Brown, S. D., & Hackett, G. (2002). Social cognitive career theory. *Career Choice and Development*, *4*(1), 255–311. http://www.borbelytiborbors.extra.hu/ZSKF/CareerDevelopment.pdf#page=276

Self-Efficacy

Hackett, G., & Betz, N. E. (1995). Self-efficacy and career choice and development. In A. Bandura (Ed.), *Self-efficacy, adaptation, and adjustment: Theory, research, and application* (pp. 249–280). Cambridge. https://www.researchgate.net/profile/Barry-Zimmerman-2/publication/247480203_Self-efficacy_and_educational_development/links/549b67770cf2b80371371ad5/Self-efficacy-and-educational-development.pdf#page=249

Self-Determination Theory

Deci, E. L., Olafsen, A. H., & Ryan, R. M. (2017). Self-determination theory in work organizations: The state of a science. *Annual Review of Organizational Psychology and Organizational Behavior*, *4*, 19–43. https://www.annualreviews.org/doi/pdf/10.1146/annurev-orgpsych-032516-113108

Solution-Focused Coaching

Burwell, R., & Chen, C. P. (2006). Applying the principles and techniques of solution-focused therapy to career counselling. *Counselling Psychology Quarterly*, *19*(2), 189–203.

System 1 and System 2

Kahneman, D. (2011). *Thinking fast and slow*. MacMillan.

Yates, J. (2015). 'The heart has its reasons that reason knows nothing of': The role of the unconscious in career decision making. *Journal of the National Institute for Career Education and Counselling*, *35*(1), 28–35. https://www.nicecjournal.co.uk/index.php/nc/article/view/280

Systems Theory Framework of Careers

Patton, W., & McMahon, M. (2015). The systems theory framework of career development: 20 years of contribution to theory and practice. *Australian Journal of Career Development*, *24*(3), 141–147. https://eprints.qut.edu.au/93732/3/93732.pdf

Patton, W., & McMahon, M. (2006). The systems theory framework of career development and counseling: Connecting theory and practice. *International Journal for the Advancement of Counselling*, *28*, 153–166. https://eprints.qut.edu.au/2621/1/2621_1.pdf

Transition Theory

Barclay, S. R. (2015). Turning transition into triumph: Applying Schlossberg's transition model to career transition. In K. Maree & A. Di Fabio (Eds), *Exploring new horizons in career counselling* (pp. 219–232). Brill.

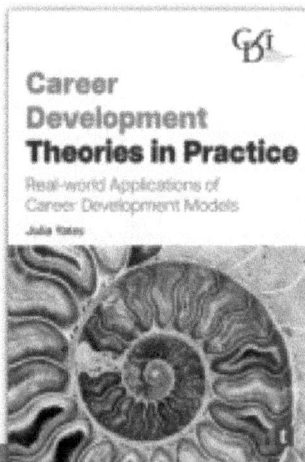